# PITTSBURGH

*REMEMBERS*

# WORLD WAR II

# PITTSBURGH
## *REMEMBERS*
# WORLD WAR II

*Dr. Joseph F. Rishel*

Charleston · London

THE
History
PRESS

Published by The History Press
Charleston, SC 29403
www.historypress.net

First published 2011

Manufactured in the United States

ISBN 978.1.60949.144.4

Library of Congress Cataloging-in-Publication Data
Pittsburgh remembers World War II / edited by Joseph F. Rishel.
p. cm.
Includes bibliographical references and index.
ISBN 978-1-60949-144-4
1. World War, 1939-1945--Pennsylvania--Pittsburgh. 2. World War, 1939-1945--Social aspects--Pennsylvania--Pittsburgh. 3. World War, 1939-1945--Personal narratives, American. 4. Oral history--Pennsylvania--Pittsburgh. 5. Interviews--Pennsylvania--Pittsburgh. 6. Soldiers--Pennsylvania--Pittsburgh--Biography. 7. Pittsburgh (Pa.)--Biography. 8. Pittsburgh (Pa.)--History--20th century. I. Rishel, Joseph Francis, 1945- II. Title: Pittsburgh remembers World War 2. III. Title: Pittsburgh remembers World War Two.
D769.85.P41P537 2011
940.53'74886--dc23
2011017848

# CONTENTS

# CONTENTS

# ACKNOWLEDGEMENTS

This book owes its existence to the efforts of the graduate students who are listed as the authors of each of the chapters and to the narrators. The graduate student authors who were selected for this book made determined efforts to capture the thoughts, emotions and experiences of those who had lived through the war, yet it was the narrators' cooperation and their willingness to be interviewed that made this book possible. These chapters were retained by the Pennsylvania Department of the Carnegie Library of Pittsburgh and transferred into electronic format by volunteer Diane Holleran under the guidance of the director, Marilyn Holt, to whom I am greatly indebted. I appreciate the efforts of my wife, Helen, who so patiently read and reread this manuscript, and of my daughter, Marjorie, for her technological assistance. I would also like to thank Duquesne University professor Dr. Perry Blatz; Thomas White, university archivist at Duquesne University; and James Duzyk of Robert Morris University for their reading, advice and encouragement. The selection of photographs was facilitated by David Grinnell, director of archives at the Senator John Heinz History Center; Gilbert Pietrzak, coordinator at the Pittsburgh Photographic Library; and Edward Galloway, director of the Archives Service Center at the University of Pittsburgh Libraries. I am grateful to Hannah Cassilly, commissioning editor, and Hilary McCullough, editorial department manager, both of The History Press, for all of their patient guidance and advice. Lastly, I would like to thank the administration of Duquesne University for their support of this project. The publication of the photographs in this book was made possible by a grant from the National Endowment for the Humanities.

# INTRODUCTION

On the first day of September 1939, residents of Allegheny County, Pennsylvania, while enjoying their annual county fair, were startled to learn that Germany had invaded Poland, thus beginning the Second World War in Europe. Two days later, Great Britain and France declared war on Germany. At the county fair, as its weeklong run continued, several thousand people gathered in a peace demonstration. The reality of violent world events intruded on the Pittsburgh area with an immediacy that the coming years would only magnify.

With a population of 671,659, Pittsburgh ranked as the tenth-largest American city in the 1940 census. It was and is the county seat of Allegheny County, which in 1940 had a population of 1,411,539, making it one of the largest and most important counties in the United States. Its importance is frequently expressed in terms of manufacturing, and correctly so, but even before World War II, the Pittsburgh area was a leader in banking, technology, food processing, electronics, chemicals, education and medicine. Yet it was, of course, an industrial powerhouse, the importance of which was known to America's enemies even as it was to Americans themselves. That power was manifesting itself to an awesome degree. Like the rest of the nation, the Pittsburgh area was struggling to climb out of the Great Depression, which had afflicted it for nearly a decade. Steel was its lifeblood, and steel-producing Pittsburgh had suffered greatly in the 1930s. Unemployment nationally had been a quarter of the nation's non-farm workforce, but with 32 percent of its workforce unemployed, Pittsburgh had been especially hard hit. A reaction was inevitable. In 1931, some 5,000 "hunger strikers" paraded through Pittsburgh city streets. The following year, at the bottom of the Depression, Father James Cox, pastor of Saint Patrick's Catholic Church in the Strip District, led an "army" of 15,000 unemployed to Washington.

By the end of 1940 it was a different story. The memory of those hungry days was only beginning to recede as the economy gained momentum and payrolls in the area picked up. Earlier that year, Congress had voted $18 billion for defense, and Pittsburgh was in for a major share of that expenditure. Every steel company in the area was operating at or near full capacity. Virtually all were planning major expansion of their facilities. By the end of 1940, business activity equaled that of 1929, the last "good" year before the Depression. In 1941, as the war raging in Europe and the Pacific drew inexorably closer to American shores, Pittsburgh's city council voted for a more stringent smoke control act, but its enforcement was postponed because of the war. A more pressing need required the Steel City's attention: military production.

On Sunday afternoon, December 7, 1941, the America First Committee, the largest group of isolationists in the country, was holding a public meeting at Soldiers and Sailors Memorial Hall in Oakland. They were there to hear the arch spokesman of isolationism, Senator Gerald Nye of North Dakota, warn of President Franklin D. Roosevelt's dangerous path of interventionism. The America Firsters alleged that Roosevelt was trying to involve the United States in the war in order to save Great Britain. As the program was about to start, some people entered the hall with the startling news that the American naval and air base at Pearl Harbor in the Hawaiian Islands had been bombed. The isolationists had heard false news stories before, and the bearers of this "false" news were unceremoniously hustled out of the hall.

The following day, many Pittsburghers were listening to radio station KDKA, the world's first commercially licensed radio broadcasting station, when President Roosevelt asked Congress for a declaration of war on Japan. Pittsburgh and the nation were aroused like never before in solid determination to win the war. Losing was not seen as an option, but no one knew that they faced three and a half years of extraordinary effort and sacrifice to accomplish that goal.

American entry into World War II abruptly ended the national debate between interventionists and isolationists. The latter group, strong in the Pittsburgh area, was labeled by some as pro-Axis. The Pittsburgh area was home to a large number of Germans and other ethnic groups that authorities had identified as subversive Nazi sympathizers. Germans were an obvious target of both the FBI and of the Pennsylvania Motor Police (i.e., the State Police), as were Italian aliens, but a less obvious Ukrainian American faction also attracted notice. Irish agents were believed to be acting on behalf of German intelligence. Communists had been tireless in the Pittsburgh area in their attempt to gain adherents. After Hitler and Stalin signed their infamous mutual nonaggression pact in August 1939, the communists became even more suspect than they had been previously. In 1940, the FBI planted Matt Cvetic—he would rise to become a recognizable name as an anti-communist during the Cold War—in the ranks of Pittsburgh-area communists as a counterspy. The communists were soon to change their pro-German stance when Hitler turned on his erstwhile ally and invaded the Soviet Union in June 1941. Neither the FBI nor the Pennsylvania Motor Police had sufficient manpower to safeguard all of the vulnerable civic, industrial and transportation soft spots against possible sabotage regardless of the perpetrators. To that end, they turned to the massive American Legion. Its members remained vigilant throughout the war and reported any suspicious activity. There was no real evidence of any acts of sabotage in Pittsburgh from any of these groups during the war. Security remained tight, however, and at times it bordered on hysteria. In 1943, some twenty-nine German aliens in the Pittsburgh area were arrested, apparently on the "evidence" that they were "guilty" of living near war plants. The average civilian, however, was unaware of these "threats," believing that everyone was working together harmoniously in a united front.

Pittsburghers were busy with the job of manufacturing war materiel and enlisting in the military: 1,200 men volunteered on the very day Roosevelt asked for a declaration of war. They would be needed. The news from the war fronts was not good. By January 1942, German submarines were sinking a ship a day off the coast of North Carolina, and by June of that year "wolf packs" of Nazi submarines had sunk four hundred Allied ships in the Atlantic. Reports from the Far East were even worse. Nearly 90,000 Americans were forced to surrender to the Japanese in the Philippines. Japan proceeded to take over much of East Asia and the western Pacific. They even occupied Alaska's Aleutian Islands. In the European Theater, the Germans were deep into Russia. In Africa, they were in Egypt and within striking distance of Great Britain's oil lifeline, the Suez Canal.

Pittsburgh's manufacturing capability played a vital role in reversing the dismal world picture. Tens of thousands of people were added to local payrolls as industrial production continued to break records. Many of these newly added workers were not originally from the area. The consequent pressure on the local housing stock was enormous. To prevent rising rental costs, in April 1942, the Pittsburgh Office of Price Administration froze rents in Allegheny County and eight surrounding counties included in the "defense rental area."

To protect the local population, in March 1942, authorities proclaimed the first of many air raid drills for Pittsburgh. In June came the first blackouts. The streetlights were darkened, and even so much as a sliver of light coming out of a home window could provoke a knock on the door from the local air raid warden. Some pointed out the foolishness of the blackouts because the glow from Pittsburgh's mills could be seen from the air for a hundred miles. Moreover, western Pennsylvania was safely behind the protection of the Appalachians and an ocean away from the battlefronts. Far from the fighting, Pittsburgh's factories worked unmolested day and night. But it was not without a price. By January 1944, the smoke from local mills, combined with the smoke from the coal-burning furnaces of homes, filled the air with a heavy "smog." It cut visibility so dramatically that thousands of war workers were unable to reach their places of employment. Much of the smoke was due to the enormous expansion of local industries. The United States Steel Homestead Works was expanded along the Monongahela River, as was the Jones and Laughlin Steel Mill in Hazelwood. Both of these expansions involved the demolition of neighboring homes, further aggravating the housing crisis. The growth of large companies changed America's workplace environment. In 1939, only 13 percent of

American workers were employed by companies having ten thousand or more employees. By 1944, that figure had grown to an astounding 30 percent of the workforce.

The war did not entirely end the tug-of-war between labor and management. Despite a no-strike pledge made by rival labor organizations American Federation of Labor and the Congress of Industrial Organizations after Pearl Harbor, there were strikes. By far the most notable was the United Mine Workers strike of 1943, when some half million miners nationwide walked off the job. The strike outraged the public, and President Roosevelt ordered a short-lived seizure of the mines. Despite the government takeover, the steel mills in Pittsburgh closed for several weeks owing to the shortage of coal. The coal strike was not indicative of the larger picture. Work stoppages accounted for only one-tenth of 1 percent of the total work time during the war. The few strikes that did occur were so-called wildcat strikes, spontaneous walkouts by workers, without sanction from union leaders.

Pittsburgh during World War II. *Senator John Heinz History Center.*

As many as twelve million men were in uniform, resulting in a severe labor shortage. Women had worked before the war and even prior to World War I, but they tended to be in low-paid, gender-specific roles. They also tended to be younger and unmarried. Frequently, getting married meant getting fired. During World War II, these restrictions loosened enormously. The number of working women in the United States grew from twelve million to eighteen million. By far, most of the new female workers were married, and a majority had children. Most important was the fact that women found work in roles heretofore held solely by males. Rosie the Riveter became a national icon. The image of a working woman flexing her muscle—a most unfeminine thing to do in the 1940s—first appeared on a poster at Westinghouse Electric and Manufacturing Company in East Pittsburgh. While commonly associated with manufacturing, Rosie appeared in many nonindustrial settings. In Pittsburgh, the first female bus drivers appeared in November 1942. Women also made advances to far higher levels. In 1942, Anne X. Alpern became Pittsburgh city solicitor, the first woman to be named to that position in a major American city. The following year, Judge Sara Soffel became the first woman to preside over an Allegheny County criminal court. After the war, the returning veterans wanted their jobs back and the number of women in local industries declined, but old limits had been tested, thus setting the stage for occupational gains two decades hence.

World War I had cost $32 billion; World War II was to cost $350 billion, with only 40 percent of that cost covered by current income. The War Revenue Act of 1942 raised taxes and lowered the threshold income for those required to pay the federal income tax. Those earning as little as $624 a year paid a 5 percent tax. Congress implemented a system of withholding from paychecks as a means of collecting it, but it was not nearly enough to pay for the war. As a result, the federal government sold war bonds, some $40 billion of them. Workers were expected to buy them. Western Pennsylvania repeatedly surpassed its "quota" of war bonds. By September 1943, the western part of the state had purchased $305 million worth of bonds, surpassing its quota by more than $6 million. Sometimes celebrities came to town to sell them. That same month the so-called Hollywood Cavalcade came to Forbes Field and sold $87 million in bonds. Even the dimes and quarters of children were sought. Seldom would they have enough money to buy a bond. Instead, they purchased stamps, which, when their little books were filled, enabled them to buy war bonds.

The bonds and the taxes would be used to support America's men and women in uniform and to equip them with the tools of victory. All told, some 15.3 million served in the Second World War. Of this number, some 5.3 million volunteered. The other 10 million were drafted. Beginning in 1940, men between the ages of twenty-one and thirty-six were required to register for the draft. After Pearl Harbor, the age was extended to men between eighteen and forty, but actual drafts in the upper age brackets were variously applied. In Allegheny County, nearly 115,000 men had registered for the draft in the two months following American entry into the war. Many thousands more would follow. For nearly all of them, the war was to be a cosmopolitanizing experience. Before the war, many Pittsburghers hadn't traveled more than a day's ride from home, much less to Europe or the Pacific. Their experiences would be life changing.

More than sixty-five years have passed since the Japanese surrendered to the United States on the USS *Missouri* in Tokyo Bay, ending World War II. That surrender closed a period of more than three and a half years of terrible carnage and bloodshed, taking some 400,000 American lives in Europe, North Africa and the Pacific. For millions of Americans who lived through World War II, whether they actually served in the military or stayed on the homefront, the war was the defining event of their lives. For many, it marked their entrance into adulthood in a world transformed beyond what anyone could have imagined. Virtually no one who lived through it remained unchanged.

# THE ORAL HISTORIES

This book is not intended to be a history of World War II. Rather, it is the collected stories of seventeen Pittsburgh-area persons as they struggled through the war years and emerged from their experiences far different than before. Most of them were young, but they all experienced the war in an intensely personal way. For some, it was their coming of age, entering as a boy or a girl and maturing into a man or woman. All felt the impact of the war and the national climate of patriotism and commitment.

The impetus for this book comes from a summer colloquium taught to graduate students from 2002 through 2008 by Dr. Joseph F. Rishel, a professor of history at Duquesne University. In that course, the topic of which was World War II, the students were taught how to conduct an oral history. They then selected persons to interview who retained vivid memories of World War II and were willing to have their narratives published. To be interviewed for this project, the person need not have actually been in the military, though most were. He or she needed only to possess memories of that war. Although some were active on the homefront, working in a defense industry, serving in civil defense or volunteering for rationing or recycling duties, others were in high school or even grade school during the war. For them, interest in the war played an important role impacting their school, family and social lives. They experienced the war through relatives and friends serving in the military, through the modern mass media of movies, radio and newspapers, through after-school work and through the shortages of consumer goods. All were caught up in very personal ways in this world cataclysm.

Their stories are as varied as the American people themselves. Each person was interviewed several times before the story could be written in term paper form by the graduate student, who acted as interviewer. Because of this, each narrative in this book has a different author, though the term "author" is used loosely here. The true authors of the wartime biographies are the men and women who told their stories. So many decades later, their stories remain remarkably bright, surprisingly clear and always interesting. Each of the biographies is unique. All have something to add to our knowledge of the most destructive war of all time. The common denominator of the contributors to this collective memory is that all are Pittsburgh-area residents. The book intends to capture a broad range of society within a limited geographical area, demonstrating vast differences in how various individuals participated in or merely coped with changes in daily life inherent to a world at war.

In editing these narratives, every effort was made to maintain the character of each interview and not to interfere with the style of the graduate student author or the mood evoked. The students reflected differing degrees of familiarity with their interview subjects. Some referred to them by surnames, others used their first names in the narratives. Quotations were kept as close to what was written as possible. The editing consists of clarifications, some supplemental information and some improvements to wording and flow, as well as a few factual corrections. The modern-day recollections of the respondents were expressed in the present tense. This was done to differentiate what persons thought or said during the war from their later memories. An attempt was made to select interviews that presented different but complementary views of the war, including those of combatants, military support personnel and a wide range of civilian situations from the Pittsburgh area.

As the wartime generation passes away, they hope to leave posterity a sense of what it was like to live during those stressful yet unifying times. They also hope that the reader will realize the sacrifices everyone made for the cause of victory. It is their desire that their stories will live forever through the publication of this book.

*Part I*

# *Those Who Served on the Homefront*

# Anywhere, Anytime—However They Could Serve

*Jean "DeDe" Barnard Anderson,*

*As told to Danae Brentzel*

Jean "DeDe" Barnard Anderson was a sixteen-year-old high school senior when the U.S. naval base at Pearl Harbor was attacked on December 7, 1941. Until that point, the petite and lively young woman with the chestnut-brown hair had been living a fairly typical existence within the small town of Larimer, Pennsylvania, located east of McKeesport. Her day-to-day life consisted of school, chores, friends and dates, the usual activities for a young woman. For DeDe, however, as with the millions of others who came of age during the war years, the entire focus and scope of her life would be altered by the events taking place thousands of miles away from her hometown.

Recollecting that day, DeDe says that she heard about the bombing in the same way as many of her friends. She had gone to see a movie that Sunday, and as she and her pals exited the theater, they were met with the news that would change the world as they knew it. She thinks that her pre–Pearl Harbor home was unusual for Larimer in that it was more focused on world events. Her father took an active interest in news reporting on Hitler's armies as they crossed international borders and conquered new territories. The Japanese, on the other hand, were not even a consideration. "Before that, I don't know that any of us really felt threatened…We were thinking about Hitler, and none of us ever thought that the Japanese would attack—it was so far away from us, I don't think we realized until the boys started going. Then it was real."

Real, indeed. In fact, DeDe still remembers the first hometown boy to be killed in action, a young man named Cornelius "Cornie" Pass. Her life, too, was undergoing changes as she graduated from high school and began to consider her future. A member of a family that prized hard work, simply sitting idle was not an option for DeDe, even if she had wanted to do so. She therefore entered Grace Martin, an academy for young women owned and operated by a Mrs. Cornelius. Located off Grant Street in downtown Pittsburgh, Grace Martin offered its young female students lessons in language and other "useful aspects of secretarial work." In addition to her schoolwork, DeDe would also go with her fellow Grace Martin girls to what she termed "a certain quota of USO dances" being held throughout the city in places like the ballroom at the William Penn Hotel. The soldiers appreciated the attention of the beautiful young women, and the dances provided an opportunity to "do their part," a desire held by all Americans, according to DeDe. Although she later had a sweetheart in the service, DeDe knew that her beau would never object to her going to the USO dances. It was simply another sign of how the post–Pearl Harbor world differed from the one that preceded it. She feels that people's attitudes had changed, and changed for the better.

The social landscape of Pittsburgh was not the only thing that changed. The changing economy and the ever-decreasing male workforce opened up opportunities that were not available prior to the war. Fueled by patriotism, the women of Pittsburgh were ready for them. DeDe was not alone in her desire to help. She says that "to become part of the war effort, many women worked in the factories; many, in addition to [their] regular jobs, served with the Red Cross, [helped] in hospitals where there were shortages, served on numerous committees, sold war bonds and attended USO functions." Everyone did the task for which he or she was best suited.

After graduation from Grace Martin, DeDe found a position working for Rosenbaum's Department Store writing patriotic jingles to be played on the radio. After a year of that, she was ready for more responsibility, and she found it at the massive Westinghouse plant in East Pittsburgh, where she worked as an executive secretary in the Industrial Relations

War fund volunteers at the Pennsylvania College for Women, now Chatham University, update a poster showing the contributions of students and faculty, 1945. *William J. Gaughan Collection, University of Pittsburgh.*

Department. During most of the remaining war years, DeDe remembers Westinghouse manufacturing various war goods. Her father, too, worked at Westinghouse. It was not uncommon for a number of family members to work in the plant. Westinghouse believed that good work habits traveled in families.

Her father did his part for the war effort and his fellow employees by sharing what he could. Living outside the city as he did, DeDe's father, Frank Barnard, was able to use the land surrounding his house for that World War II phenomenon, the victory garden. DeDe remembers, "Victory Gardens were in evidence everywhere. If you had property, you had one. Some areas in a community were mutually shared and tended by many. These gardens were hand-spaded, and nothing was sold. Vegetables were given to those unable to garden, and all shared freely in the bounty. For instance, my dad, who worked at Westinghouse, had co-workers from the urban areas come out and share the available harvest each week." During the Depression years of the 1930s, Frank had also generously shared the produce from his large garden with his co-workers.

Bustling with the production of war goods, Westinghouse was certainly an exciting place to work during the war years. Each of its workers, from executives to secretaries to those on the production line, could be sure of putting in a hard day's work. Despite the grueling schedule, at the end of their shifts many volunteered their time and efforts elsewhere to help the war effort. DeDe took the train each day at the end of her shift from Pittsburgh to Greensburg, where she went to the hospital to put in her time as a nurse's aide. Much as her father was her connection at Westinghouse, DeDe also had a contact at the hospital. Her mother, Nelle, worked as a head nurse there. A former World War I army nurse who had served near the front lines in France, Nelle knew both the horrors of war and the importance of a homefront for those fighting it. She had

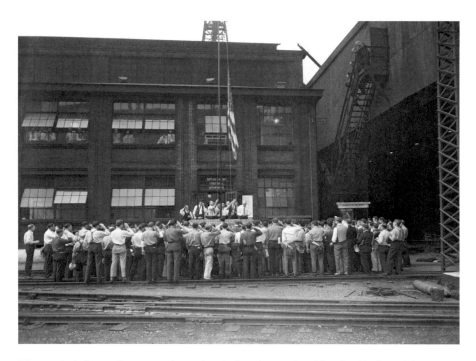

The patriotic fervor that swept the nation during the war is evident in this flag-raising ceremony at a Pittsburgh plant. Note the workers saluting in military style rather than placing their hands over their hearts. *William J. Gaughan Collection, University of Pittsburgh.*

passed on this legacy to her daughter. DeDe recalled that the hospital was a bustling place; after all, wartime doesn't stop civilian life entirely. However, there were shortages, such as bandages and some medications, which made hospital work difficult at times. Busy, busy days and busy, busy nights. Though DeDe had little unclaimed time, she didn't mind. It was all, again, a part of doing what she could to help.

DeDe remembers the traveling she did during the war with a wry laugh, not because of the destinations, but because of the means of travel. As many other western Pennsylvanians did during the war years, DeDe took an early train to and from East Pittsburgh for work each day. To travel a longer distance to visit a friend taking a naval V-5 course at Franklin and Marshall College, she took the train as well. None of her friends who owned cars were able to obtain enough ration coupons to buy gasoline,

The July 4, 1945 issue of the *Pittsburgh Post-Gazette* remonstrated wartime travelers. "While soldiers thumb rides or stand in jam-packed trains and buses, the civilian population continues to take 'essential' trips, despite the warning of the Office of Defense Transportation." *Carnegie Library of Pittsburgh.*

so the train was really their only option. It was not a comfortable means of transport by any stretch of the imagination, for most of the traditional "passenger" cars had been commandeered by the military for transport of troops and equipment.

For civilians, she remembers, cattle cars had been fitted with benches for the traveling "comfort" (again the wry smile here!) of the passengers. However, those who managed to find a seat on the cattle car benches were the lucky ones. The other passengers did the best they could by sitting on the piles of luggage between coaches. Not the most relaxing way to travel, certainly, though one does suspect that these seating arrangements encouraged the passengers to make an extra effort to be early for the train.

The loss of a seat on the train was of minor importance compared to another, far more pressing deficiency in DeDe's life. Like millions of other fashion-conscious women, rationing hit her hard. In her recollection, *everything* was rationed—silk stockings, butter, meat, shoes, gasoline, sugar, metal appliances, etc. Not only that, to try to trade one's ration coupons for

With gasoline rationing and the consequent rise in demand for public transportation, Pittsburgh Railways called back into service streetcars such as this one from 1924. *Carnegie Library of Pittsburgh.*

these and many other items, each buyer had to stand in seemingly "endless" lines, sometimes only to find that the item in question had been bought out moments before. Many Americans, however, found ways around the rationing system, and the most popular of those routes was the black market.

Pittsburgh, too, had those who "could get what you needed for enough money." DeDe recalls a man on whom everyone relied for black market coupons. The man—even after all these years she declined to give his name—could provide coupons for literally everything, provided one had the cash to pay for it. Some Westinghouse employees patronized the black market for little items like sugar, butter and especially cigarettes, which had virtually disappeared from the aboveground market. Though not actually rationed, a tobacco quota was reserved for the military.

DeDe's most memorable experience with the black market, however, didn't involve something as trivial as cigarettes. It involved something far more important to a fashion-conscious girl: shoes. Though she couldn't remember what she had paid for the black market shoe coupons, DeDe does remember that it was an exorbitant amount of money. She chuckles as she recalled her excitement when she took the precious coupons home to show her family. Her father, an avid supporter of the president and of the war effort, was furious. He took DeDe's coupons and—horror of horrors!—burned them in an ashtray right before her eyes, instructing her that she was never to bring black market items into his house ever again. Despite her heartbroken cry of "You burned my *shoes!*" Frank remained inflexible; DeDe never again purchased black market clothing coupons. Cigarettes, however, were another story.

The rest of the rationing DeDe remembers almost cheerfully. Coffee was a scarce commodity, so the Barnard family drank chicory instead. What they called "butter" was actually a whitish margarine made yellow through the addition of orange coloring in a small capsule. Once the capsule in the bag of margarine was ruptured, DeDe would massage the color throughout the bag, causing the substance to turn yellow. The margarine, unlike today's spreads, had a distinctive taste, which made it a poor substitute for butter. The shortages were not a crushing daily disappointment. The Barnard family had just weathered the Great Depression, and they all knew that these small sacrifices meant that they were once again helping with the war effort, even in this small way.

Not all aspects of the war made for cheery reflections, however. One of the most difficult things DeDe remembers was the sheer lack of information they had about loved ones serving overseas. "News from afar was limited to fireside chats by FDR, radio, newsreels in theaters and newspapers. Communication with our loved ones took the form of V-mail letters, and much was blacked out by censorship except for 'ifs, ands & buts.' No hourly 'on-spot' coverage as today—perhaps a blessing in its way." One of the V-mail letters DeDe received looked like a black-and-white patchwork quilt. The pens of the censors had blacked out all that might indicate where the writer was and what he was doing.

Other memories were more cheerful, including visits to relatives in the Washington, D.C./Baltimore area. Naval Academy balls at Annapolis were among the highlights of DeDe's wartime social memories. The excitement and tension surrounding the nation's capital were palpable. There were also luncheons at the Iron Cross Inn and, perhaps most exciting for this avid lover of animals, visits to the compound where dogs were trained for special service. At that time, this was the best part of her

Jean "DeDe" Bernard Anderson.
*Jean Bernard Anderson.*

visits. She recalls, "My memories of that time I spent in the 'magical' surroundings of Washington didn't mean much, being very young," but were certainly exciting nonetheless.

Some members of DeDe's family even played a part in one of the most controversial decisions of the war. In 1945, DeDe's aunt, Lorraine Barnard Hobday, served in the Truman administration, working as an assistant for Robert Nathan, chief economic stabilizer and author of the book *Mobilizing for Abundance*. DeDe often visited both Lorraine and her Aunt Elsie and uncle (affectionately called "Doc") at their homes in Silver Spring, Maryland, and in Baltimore. As the story goes, in late July or early August 1945, DeDe's mother and Aunt Chris were staying with Lorraine for a short vacation. One day, Lorraine invited Nelle and Chris to go "along for a ride" as she delivered some mail for her boss. After the atomic bomb was dropped a few days later on Hiroshima, the astonished Pittsburghers learned that the letters Lorraine had been hand-delivering were notices to the various key members of the Truman administration apprising them of the government's intention to bomb Hiroshima. Shocked, Chris burst out, "Jesus Christ! I thought they had a whole bucket of them!" Still, as far as DeDe ever knew, they never spoke of it again, and she doubts that the importance of what they had been a part of ever occurred to these two unsophisticated ladies. DeDe was not along for that fateful ride. She had been sent home to Pittsburgh by her concerned uncle. Doc, whose job was affiliated with the yet-to-be formed CIA, felt that the naval boys in Baltimore would "tear the town apart" with the coming victory and this was an atmosphere far too racy (and potentially dangerous) for his young niece.

Before leaving Baltimore for Pittsburgh, however, DeDe had two rather unusual experiences. The hotel where she stayed was very near Aberdeen Proving Grounds and also housed many young men. She assumed they were involved in wartime intelligence. She recalls seeing several of them one day in naval uniforms, the next dressed as army privates and then in nondescript civilian clothes. That was certainly unusual had they been civilians. However, the experience she found most odd happened one night as she lay in bed reading. The novel was *Forever Amber*, and as DeDe found it most uninteresting, she found herself idly looking out her window at the water below. She could see a boat with lights and clearly visible people on its deck. Suddenly, as she watched it, the boat "vanished," much to her surprise. When she reported the incident to Doc the next morning, he dismissed it. Years later, she learned that scientists at Aberdeen Proving Grounds had been involved with plans to disguise boats so that they would seemingly vanish. Today, she believes that she may have inadvertently seen a test run of the experiment, though she can never be sure. As DeDe says, "Time does have a way of removing many salient details. So it is with all of us, trying, trying to remember things which will remain forever ambiguous shadows."

After the war ended, DeDe eventually went to work at U.S. Steel as a secretary. Even into the early 1950s, the effects of the war were still being felt. She recalls a room in the basement of a downtown building, possibly the Union Trust Building, where an enormous map was located. The purpose of this map and room was to plot overhead aircraft—any aircraft. When a "suspicious" plane was spotted, DeDe recalls that all of the civilian personnel had to leave the room immediately. Clearly, though the war was over, the world had changed.

Recalling what it was like to live in Pittsburgh during the war, DeDe says, "We didn't become immune or apathetic because we weren't bombarded hourly by the horrors really existing. We on the homefront played the waiting game and, at the war's end, experienced the wonderful anticipation of recovery from the loneliness created by the war years, and joyous reunions with those who witnessed much that we could not be part of ever. That would always remain a road untraveled."

Today, DeDe Anderson is a woman who has lived a life no less rich and full than the one she lived during the war years. The "hats" she has worn are varied: wife, mother, writer, model, secretary, animal rescue worker—you name it, DeDe has tried it. The legacy of service to others, passed down by her parents and perfected during the war years, is one she has passed on to her own child and grandchildren, as well as her nieces. When asked about the spirit of those on the homefront during the war, DeDe says that each man and woman gave of himself or herself "anywhere, anytime—however they could serve." Her life has been a model of this motto, and in her recollections of the war years, its foundation can clearly be seen.

# IT WAS A TERRIBLE BUT ROMANTIC THING

*Richard Charles Martin,*

*As told to Jo Ellen Aleshire*

Richard Charles Martin was a young man who did not consider himself anything but ordinary. Countless others of his generation felt the same way. But most of them, in an extraordinary way, gave what was needed at the time and then, almost casually, went on to raise a family and lead a life of merit, with faith, values and hopes intact.

Richard Charles "Dick" Martin was born on December 4, 1927, and much to his chagrin, was almost too young to actively participate in World War II. As a young man still in high school during most of the war, he "wanted to fly but I lived too late. You had the urgency that 'I have to go.' We really didn't know what we were getting into. But that urgency was out there. It was very all encompassing, this war atmosphere. Then when you started to see so many men in uniform, it was almost overwhelming. You knew we were at war." The war changed "boring, lazy summer days" into days where he says everything seemed to "become accelerated" and "the fighting and the war effort overtook everyone's lives." Although he vividly remembers the heaviness, the dark days and tragedies of the war, he was also enamored by the total war effort, both at home and abroad, and was young enough to entertain the romance of it.

Dick, along with his younger sister, Nancy, lived with their banker father, Charles Martin, and homemaker mother, Pauline Zeigler Martin, in Ambridge, Pennsylvania, about five miles down the Ohio River from Pittsburgh. In Ambridge, the majority of families were staunch Democrats and ethnic blue-collar steelworkers. Dick's parents, however, were part of an old dyed-in-the-wool Republican family who, with a German ancestry, were now third-generation Americans. Ancestors on his mother's side had fought in the Civil War. The Depression had not changed their way of life significantly because the bank where his father was an officer continued to thrive and "we were not a big family. We were fairly privileged in a lot of ways." As supporters of Wendell Willkie and Thomas Dewey, they were initially alarmed when President Roosevelt chose to run for unprecedented third and fourth terms. They were, however, very patriotic and had an interventionist stance concerning the war. To this day, Dick, as his parents had done, has always proudly flown the American flag outside his home in South Park, Pennsylvania, making sure to treat it with the proper respect he learned from them, with the respect he derived from growing up during the Depression era that produced hardworking, principled people and with the respect for his country that was created by his coming of age during World War II.

Dick and his family were in their car driving to visit his aunt in Steubenville, Ohio, when they heard about the attack on Pearl Harbor on the car radio. "There are certain events in your life you remember. It was a black day." Not knowing specifically where Pearl Harbor was, throughout the rest of the war Dick relied on his globe and "learned a lot of geography of places you never heard of…Yugoslavia with Tito and all…Anzio beach…[Monte] Casino where the big monastery was being bombed…the rescue operation at Dunkirk. On D-Day I can remember my mother coming up and waking me up and saying they had invaded Europe." The radio provided Dick with daily contact about the war: FDR's "Day of Infamy" speech and other fireside chats conjured up for Dick the image of FDR as "such a big man, even though he was crippled. He was just such a presence." Other memories include heroic Winston Churchill's "rallying cry" to the steadfast, besieged British people and the smoky voice of Edward R. Murrow broadcasting from London with "bombing going on all around" and reporting about blitzkriegs, blackouts, gas masks and subway tunnels.

Newspapers were both "propaganda and patriotic" in their coverage. They presented daily accounts of the action in Europe and the Pacific and of atrocities committed by the enemy. Movietone newsreels were another source of news for Dick. Vivid footage of actual battles and events was shown prior to viewing patriotic war movies. Dick reminisces about some favorites, such as Greer Garson's *Mrs. Miniver*, Robert Taylor's *Back to Bataan*, Randolph Scott's *Gung Ho* and the John Wayne movies that flooded the screens. Dick also enjoyed the big musicals that provided a respite from the war. Three actors that Dick recalls who

In 1942, the U.S. Steel Homestead Works entrance was enhanced with flags flying like the halyard of a ship. Note the Navy E Award flag. The Homestead Works produced eighty-two million tons of 160-inch steel plate for the navy. *William J. Gaughan Collection, University of Pittsburgh.*

added to the patriotic fervor were Jimmy Stewart, who enlisted, flew countless missions and eventually became a colonel; Clark Gable, who enlisted in the U.S. Army Air Corps; and Tyrone Power. Dick was told by a college roommate, who had served as a USMC pilot with Power, that off-screen he was not well liked and was "quite egotistical." Dick particularly remembers one of the first patriotic songs written about the war, "Remember Pearl Harbor," and remarked that the *Pittsburgh Sun-Telegraph*, a Hearst newspaper, published the words on the front page for years on the anniversary of the attack.

Dick's mother thought that he, like all members of the younger generation, was being rebellious in listening to "big band" music. It was a far cry from her fondness for the old Victrola recordings of opera tenor Enrico Caruso. Glenn Miller's band, Dick's favorite, could be heard on the radio every Saturday night, and he felt a great loss and sadness when Miller's plane was shot down during the war while he was traveling to entertain the troops.

Dick's father was an air raid warden in the "800 block, Maplewood Street." When the local fire station alarm sounded a warning, he would don his white hat and police the area, checking that blinds had been pulled and that all lights were out. Each air raid warden was given an identification poster with enemy planes and battleships silhouetted in black. As a young man, Dick took great pride in learning all about Messerschmidts, Heinkels, Junkers, P-40s and P-51s from those silhouettes. He bought war bonds, one $0.25 stamp at a time, until completing an $18.75 savings "book," convertible to a war bond that would then reach $25.00 upon maturity.

He and his father were active in the Boy Scouts, and his troop collected wire hangers, tin, paper, anything to help the war effort. Awful-tasting oleomargarine that was mixed with a yellow coloring instead of real butter and using red and blue tokens to buy rationed meat and sugar are distinct memories also. There were no new rubber tires for civilians, and gas was rationed, so Dick's family would travel by train instead of car on Saturdays from Ambridge to Pittsburgh. On those trips into the city Dick saw "uniforms everywhere." There was "so much prosperity during the war" because of all the war production factories and manufacturing jobs, including those popularized by Rosie the Riveter. The streets were

# Those Who Served on the Homefront

Promotional displays for the sale of war bonds sometimes included attention-getting devices such as these inflatables shown here in Pittsburgh's Strip District. *Carnegie Library of Pittsburgh.*

Industrial districts frequently featured billboards exhorting the workers not to miss a day on the job. This one at the U.S. Steel Homestead Works, April 1943, was locally produced by Pittsburgh's Cy Hungerford. *William J. Gaughan Collection, University of Pittsburgh.*

"swarming with people on Saturday nights going to Murphy's [five and ten cent store] and all different places," but no one could forget the reality of the war. "Everywhere there were signs of a call to patriotism and the need to fight the enemy." The ethos of the homefront was one of unity for the war effort, sacrifice and doing the right thing, juxtaposed against a sense of an awakening and exhilaration after years of the Depression.

Dick's high school gym class was reconstructed to resemble a military training obstacle course with vigorous calisthenics. Returning students would come back in their uniforms and show off their physical prowess. Dick was especially in awe of a paratrooper who did one-arm pushups. For his high school senior prom, Dick bartered to obtain a B gas rationing card instead of his father's lower-ranking A card, which allowed him only three to four gallons, so that he would have enough gas to take his date to the prom. The B card entitled the holder up to eight gallons per week. There were other categories: C for those deemed essential to the war effort, H for agricultural use, T for truckers and X providing an unlimited supply of gasoline for essential personnel such as civil defense workers and the clergy. His girlfriends (but not his mother) painted lines up the back of their legs to simulate the seams on the silk stockings they could no longer buy.

The steel mills near Dick's home—Jones & Laughlin, Wyckoff Steel and A.M. Byers—provided another form of entertainment for young people who watched the lights emanating from their Bessemer converters. "Well, we loved to go up there at night and it was just throwing this big glow all over the neighborhood up there." Steel, iron and glass production in Pittsburgh had always been a booming business. But the lend-lease policy of "trips over the ocean up to Murmansk up in Russia...we were feeding Russia and giving supplies" and the United States entry into the war caused Pittsburgh's war production to grow dramatically. Steel mills and manufacturing companies were revamped to meet the high demand of war supplies and machinery. On one occasion, Dick recalled that the famous boxer Barney Ross, while conducting "PR for the marines" in Pittsburgh, presented Spang Chalfant Pipe Mill with a government "E" award and flag to display for its outstanding war production of cannon shells.

Playing in the high school band provided Dick with some of his most engaging and vivid memories. His band often played for the christening and launching of new landing ship tanks (LSTs), which were

# Those Who Served on the Homefront

Pittsburgh companies worked hard to achieve the coveted Army-Navy E Award given by the military for meeting production quotas. The pennants, bestowed with great fanfare, were flown with the American flag and encouraged wartime enthusiasm to produce still more. *Senator John Heinz History Center.*

amphibious ships that carried vehicles, tanks and troops to beachhead landings, including the D-Day invasion. In his own town of Ambridge, the American Bridge Company transformed a whole section of its former bridge and barge-building area down near the Ohio River and built a shipyard "by hauling dirt out of the hillside of the little town of Fair Oaks." His band played for celebratory launchings on Neville Island where the Dravo Corporation manufactured LSTs and "a little patrol boat that was called a DE [destroyer escort] and looked like a junior destroyer."

Immediately upon graduation from Ambridge High School at the age of seventeen, Dick's determination finally persuaded his parents to "sign" for him, granting their permission for his enlistment, since he was under the legal age of eighteen. He knew that the war was winding

A large crowd assembled for the launching of the USS *Jenks*, the first of twenty-eight destroyer escorts built by the Dravo Corporation on Neville Island, September 11, 1943. *Carnegie Library of Pittsburgh.*

down, and if he were to participate, he could not wait until his eighteenth birthday in December 1945 to enlist. Early in the war Dick dreamed of being a pilot, but now he realized "you couldn't get into the air force to become a pilot; they didn't need you anymore." His attempt to enlist in the coast guard was thwarted by a temporary liver disorder, and he was physically disqualified. With excitement and genuine patriotism, Dick enlisted in the navy in July 1945. V-E Day had already occurred, and Dick remembers the "whooping it up" on the streets and everyone hugging everyone else in celebration of victory in Europe. However, there was still the Pacific Theater to be won and the possibility of an invasion of Japan, so enlistment continued. The old Pittsburgh Post Office on Smithfield Street was where all draftees and enlistees stripped down for their physicals. Dick passed this time, although he laughs recalling how the doctor never could get his knees to react to his continued tapping.

# Those Who Served on the Homefront

The old post office on Smithfield Street, dating to 1891, was pressed into service as the principal recruiting, induction and physical examination center for tens of thousands of Pittsburgh inductees. *Senator John Heinz History Center.*

While waiting for the call up to serve, he applied to Penn State in case he was not called, and he worked part time at the Ambridge Auto Parts Shop. Finally in October the call came. It was after the dropping of the bombs on Hiroshima and Nagasaki and following V-J Day. The war was essentially over. Dick had agreed with Truman's decision to use the atomic bomb. "We were told that over a million soldiers and civilians would have died if we had invaded, so I had no qualms in what he [Truman] did. It didn't sound nice and you couldn't help but feel that it was a terrible thing. But you still had that presence of that generation that it was necessary. Everybody hated the Japanese. That's war and the mindset of that time. That was *the* enemy." If the bombs had not been dropped, Dick, doubtless, would have been part of the invasion of Japan. Meanwhile, soldiers were still needed for the restructuring and occupation of Germany and Japan and for all types of service units. Dick

Just as it had served as a point of debarkation for Pittsburgh's World War I military, the old Baltimore and Ohio Railroad Station on the Monongahela was a point of departure in World War II. *Senator John Heinz History Center.*

strongly acknowledges that the "fellows on the front lines were serviced by so many people." Even though his time in the navy was postwar service, he knew it was necessary to the total war effort.

Leaving for boot camp from the old Baltimore and Ohio Railroad Station along the downtown bank of the Monongahela River, Dick was sent to Camp Peary near Williamsburg, Virginia, in October 1945.

He was assigned to Company 748, B-1, and became a navy amphibious seaman. The base and barracks were the condemned remnants of a former Seabees training camp. Dick calls the barracks "tar paper shacks" because of the half-destroyed potbellied stoves, inadequate doors and whistling wind through the huge cracks in the walls that could only be muffled by placing mattresses all around. The rickety bunks were of concern to 130-pound Dick, as his top bunkmate weighed over 200 pounds. The unit underwent the navy's complete ten weeks of training, including riflery, rowing exercises on the shallow James River (which to Dick seemed somewhat superfluous) and marching, marching, marching. He was thrilled to be in the navy but at times could not help thinking that the training was "sort of a postwar afterthought." German POWs were secretly kept at Camp Peary, and although Dick did not converse with them due to language barriers, they acted as pastry chefs. "No matter how bad the main meal was, once we got the cake, everything was wonderful." His Christmas Day 1945 was spent scrubbing and then "kayaking" wood on wood to create a shine on the library floor.

After basic training, half of his unit was dispatched from the OGU (outgoing unit) to Japan, while Dick, now seaman first class, was sent to Astoria, Oregon, which was a little fishing village on the Columbia River about 150 miles north of the Portland shipyards. He was commissioned to a LSM 116 (landing ship, medium), which had returned from the invasion of Okinawa. The LSM was designed as a more compact and maneuverable ship than the larger LST.

Dick's primary job in the navy during his ten months of service (October 1945 through August 1946) was to participate in one of those invaluable service units. While not receiving any of the glory of being involved in heroic action, his service was a necessary part of implementing the "deconstruction" of the war. His unit was responsible for mothballing the landing craft fleet. Mothballing involved cleaning the bilges and dehumidifying the compartments. Guns were wrapped in waterproof paper. The entire ship was cleaned and then it was towed down to Portland's shipyards, where the hulls were sprayed with red clay for a protective covering. The work "was kind of interesting, but you wondered what you were doing when you found out that eventually they all disappeared." After being on the deck crew for a while, Dick was named a temporary yeoman and wrote up discharge papers for returning LSM sailors from the Pacific who shared their tales of the fighting. Dick speaks fondly of a gentleman who befriended some of the men in their unit and fed them good home-cooked meals. They whiled away their free time playing basketball, using a basket positioned on the side of the tank storage area of his LSM. "Someone had to get the rowboat out and row down the river to recover the basketball when it went overboard."

After ten months, the navy decided to "get rid of us." Dick was not in the navy long enough to rise above the rank of seaman first class. While he chose to return home to enter college at Penn State, an alternative for extended service was given to the men in his unit. If Dick had joined the "enlistments for a ship called the USS *Dixie*," he would have been sent to Bikini Island, where postwar nuclear testing was being conducted. "The fellows who enlisted didn't know they were going to have aftereffects years later," Dick muses.

Dick applied to and was accepted at Penn State. Many of the GI Bill college students were much older than Dick and had more war experience, but on the whole, Dick feels that he and the other veterans took their studies more seriously than the recent high school graduates. Many freshmen were shipped out to the state system of teachers' colleges, so Dick attended Slippery Rock for one year and then completed his degree as a business major at Penn State Main. Dick feels that the classes were rigorous, but some of the professors, due to a lack of adequate faculty following the war, were required to teach courses that were not in their field.

Ironically, at the end of college, Dick was again called up for military duty in the Korean War, but he never served. He has been honorably discharged from two wars, while never serving in battle. Rumors also began to emerge that two new world powers following World War II, the United States and the USSR, could make the "Cold War hot," and Dick thought there just might be a chance for a third call to war.

Dick still has his navy uniforms, but he laughingly notes it was a wonder he could ever fit into them. He remembers the difficulty of dressing with thirteen buttons on the pants and the lack of a zipper or buttons on the top. The Navy Amphibious Insignia was sewn on the left shoulder and the Navy Honorable Discharge Insignia on the right shoulder. Honorably discharged military were allowed to wear their uniforms for up to thirty days after discharge, so this insignia kept the MPs from thinking they were AWOL. Dick laughingly explains how the military personnel thought the eagle inside a wreath more aptly resembled a ruptured duck, so it became "the ruptured duck insignia," a term that hardly seems "honorable."

Dick Martin has maintained friendships with several of his shipmates through the ensuing years. However, he says the highlight for many men "was their time in the service, and they will talk about that until the day they die." To Dick, "it was a different era...and I wouldn't trade it for the world. I can't give the same thing to our grandkids. Maybe our kids got a little bit of it, but not the grandkids. I can't give it back to them." Dick attributed the homefront unity, the discipline learned in the navy and working as a unit on the LSM 116 as major contributing factors in his outlook on life. He became a district manager for UGI Propane Company and, after retirement, opened an office supply store with his sons. He has been happily married for fifty-four years to Jeanne Cromie. They have raised three sons and two daughters and actively participate in the care and nurturing of their eight grandchildren. All their children live nearby, and family get-togethers are treasured. Dick always has a history book in hand, and he is a Civil War buff. He has continued working part time after his second retirement and on his eightieth birthday was still a docent at the Frick Art and Historical Center in Pittsburgh. His patriotism and love of his country are as strong and vigorous—however, perhaps not quite as idealistic—as that of the young seventeen-year-old boy yearning to be part of the Second World War.

# WORLD WAR II IN THE "ROCKS"

*Nora Mulholland,*

As told to Marian Mulholland

The events that occurred in 1939 forever changed the history of the world and of millions of people in dramatic, often violent ways. They also changed the lives of those who never suffered directly from combat. While military powers gathered in preparation for large-scale clashes, in Pittsburgh, Pennsylvania, a young woman named Nora King had no idea that she, too, would face the challenges of World War II. The second youngest of nine girls, Nora was still living at the family home in McKees Rocks, just west of Pittsburgh, when the United States entered the war. Having finished high school, she had found a position working as a clerk in the employment office in downtown Pittsburgh.

At the age of twenty-one, Nora was focusing on beginning her life as an adult and therefore was mostly ignorant of the struggle that loomed in Europe until a lighthearted family excursion was soured by the realities of the global political scene. Nora first heard about the war beginning in Europe while on a family picnic at Kennywood Park one sunny September day in 1939. A park employee announced Germany's invasion of Poland over the loudspeaker. "There were many German and Polish immigrants at the park, and everyone suddenly got very quiet," Nora says. While there was no demonstrative reaction, either positive or negative, from the crowd, Nora and her family first sensed trouble was brewing for America, too.

After hearing of the outbreak of war overseas, a discernible tension began to grow in the United States. Nora found that the families in the ethnically diverse neighborhoods of Pittsburgh followed the news of German advances very carefully. Though their family ties to the old country remained, Nora believed that the trouble in Europe was something that would stay overseas. "Everyone knew the war was in Europe, but we never thought it would come to us." Yet it did. On Sunday, December 7, 1941, when the attack on Pearl Harbor occurred, Nora was at church with her family. As the family walked home, this was the only topic of conversation among themselves and all whom they met on the way. They spent the rest of the day glued to the radio, listening to the commentary. When President Roosevelt delivered his famed "Day of Infamy" speech to Congress and the nation, Nora was again at church. This time, it was during her lunch hour, and Nora joined her fellow Catholic co-workers at Mass at St. Mary's downtown. Again, she learned of world-changing events from those around her on her way back to work, and the office became quiet as employees gathered around the radio as the realization sunk in that war had begun.

The day after Pearl Harbor, headlines such as this appeared in every American newspaper. Not wishing to disclose the actual number killed in the attack (2,400), government officials understated the true extent of the nation's losses. *Carnegie Library of Pittsburgh.*

As a young woman, Nora need not fear the draft. But as she was already employed, she did not seek to obtain any of the new positions the war opened up for women. Once war was declared, her "mother [was] never so glad they had nine girls." Their father was too old to be drafted, so the immediate family did not need to fear receiving death notices by telegram, as so many nearby families did. This did not mean the Kings were spared the sorrow of losing someone important to them in combat or seeing them sent off under the draft. Some male cousins close to the family were drafted. Those relatives who entered military service all stayed in the United States, far from the fighting. One cousin, Joe Jordan, chose to join the navy and was posted in Chicago uneventfully for the duration of the war. Eddie Hess, Nora's brother-in-law, was less fortunate in his assignment. Drafted and sent to Georgia, the army took advantage of Eddie's medical training and placed him in charge of returning soldiers suffering from "battle fatigue" or post-traumatic stress disorder. "He was miserable." Whatever he witnessed, Eddie never spoke of it, but the family did come to realize that his duties took an emotional rather than physical toll on his health.

Other families Nora knew were not so lucky. "Almost all the young men I went to school with were drafted." One young man by the name of Gregoritch, a "foreigner" (in Nora's parlance, a young man born to Polish immigrants) with whom she had attended school, was sent to the Pacific. Nora became his pen pal and wrote to him throughout the war. From their correspondence, Nora came to believe that Gregoritch had some romantic feelings for her, but she did not reciprocate. Though their letters continually crossed the ocean from the time Gregoritch was deployed until he returned home, the relationship dissolved upon his return with no great deal of regret from either party.

Nora also had an undisclosed "crush" whose movements she followed with great concern. This young man was another classmate named Tom Lyons who was drafted and sent to England. Before the war, he had often walked her home after school, as he lived only a few doors away. Though she did not communicate with Lyons as she did with Gregoritch, Nora nevertheless followed his deployments secondhand through news from his family. Unlike her Pacific correspondent, Lyons did not make it home alive. A member of the U.S. Army Air Corps, Lyons was killed in 1944 in a firefight over the English Channel just before the invasion of Normandy.

Although there was a continuous stream of announcements of deaths, injuries and other heartbreaking stories to those at home, for the most part Nora remembers a sense of optimism regarding the war itself. No one imagined that defeat was a possibility. Morale remained high, and those on the homefront engaged in a variety of activities to become part of the "total war" effort. When the Battle of the Bulge occurred in 1944, Nora thought, for the first time, that the United States might actually lose the war. Despite the somewhat grim outlook that seeped into the community as the war raged, life on the homefront continued, but in a more somber fashion. Throughout the war and its attendant emotional and personal stresses, Nora continued to work in the employment office. She took advantage of the spaces left vacant by draftees at local universities to further her education. In 1943, she enrolled for two years of night school at Duquesne University and began to pursue her bachelor's degree while working to help support her family.

Though the draft demanded a continuous stream of young men, there was also a demand at home for skilled laborers for the war industries. In the employment office, Nora found her job shifting from

Workers bow their heads in prayer during a plant assembly. Such gatherings were common occurrences throughout the war. *William J. Gaughan Collection, University of Pittsburgh.*

white-collar placements to more technically skilled positions such as machinists and welders. Nora's job also evolved to specialize in recruiting people to build landing ship tanks (LSTs) on Neville Island, such as those used during the D-Day invasion of France. There was no shortage of people volunteering for shipbuilding duties, as this type of work provided an exemption from the draft. Women also found employment in Pittsburgh's booming defense industries, though typically not in manual labor–intensive positions. Nora's sister Nellie found a secretarial position at the Neville Island Works that she kept throughout the war.

The serious nature of the work occurring at Neville Island was sometimes buried under its more social aspects. The launches of new LSTs provided an opportunity for those left at home to mingle and celebrate. Nora, Nellie and other unattached young women frequently

The launching of an LST on Neville Island was cause for great celebration, complete with band and chorus. Note the Army-Navy E Award in the top tier of the grandstand, which itself was a permanent fixture at the naval yard. *Senator John Heinz History Center.*

attended the launches along with the naval officers' wives and the few single men left at home. All of the sisters who were still unmarried and living at home spent their leisure time bowling. The young women of McKees Rocks and the older men who were turned away from service formed a cross-generational league that helped keep their minds off the struggle in which they did not have a direct role.

The labor shortage created by the draft offered new economic opportunities for her family. As women began to enter the workplace, the King family joined in the female employment surge. Nora's sister, Florence, got a job at Mellon Bank. She was possibly the first female accountant the bank ever hired. "The war gave the Irish and Italian families a way into the banking business. They [the banks] had to take them because of the labor shortage caused by the draft," says Nora.

During the war, the family bought a lot of bonds. In the long run, this turned out to be a good investment. The family used the funds from the bonds to provide medical care for their father after his retirement. Sustaining the family also became more difficult in light of the efforts to support the war. While all the girls worked to pay for their own clothes and nonessential items, rationing caused problems at home. Their mother could not get enough butter for her recipes and would routinely trade sugar credits for butter stamps to get all the items she needed. Despite the inconvenience and the difficulty in obtaining certain food staples, the family never went hungry and even had access to fresh produce. The King family had a victory garden with a neighbor, Joe Graff. He plowed and portioned out a section of a three-acre lot on Pittsburgh's North Side for the girls to use. There they grew potatoes, tomatoes, lettuce and cabbage. The girls tended the garden in shifts, two or three times per week. Some were more enthusiastic about it than others. Nora says, "Florence couldn't stand it, but Nellie loved to spend time in the garden."

In addition to the "patriotic" produce, the King girls sought to do their duty in more direct ways. Five of the girls volunteered and served as air raid wardens. They were trained in the proper procedures and issued the full air raid equipment, including some helmets Nora loathed. They participated in a few small-scale drills, but as the war never reached American soil, the girls did not have any actual raids to supervise.

Students from a vocational agriculture course at Westinghouse High School harvest lettuce at their victory garden in Frick Park, June 1943. *Carnegie Library of Pittsburgh.*

Although she experienced the news of Pearl Harbor as traumatic and distressing, Nora did not experience strong emotional responses as the war drew to a close in 1945. Even the dropping of the atom bomb was more remote to young Nora than the impact of Pearl Harbor had been. As the war was winding down, the work Nora had taken on while the young men embarked on campaigns around the world became the main focus of her life. After the war, the employment office changed its role to the unemployment office. The focus was no longer on finding people to fill positions but rather on finding positions for returning soldiers. The work also changed in scale and focus. The flood of returning men meant that fewer women sought employment. Work became centered on administrating so-called 52-20s, a benefit plan for returning soldiers. The soldiers received as much as twenty dollars per week for up to a year to ensure they would not find themselves in dire financial straits. The great number of returning soldiers

Although the Times Square photograph of V-J Day celebrations was widely popularized, similar scenes, such as this one in downtown Pittsburgh, occurred in every American city. *Carnegie Library of Pittsburgh.*

also affected Nora's education. As the veterans returned, the GI Bill caused a great influx of male students. She decided not to continue her education.

The only images that remain in her mind of the war's end were those splashed on the front pages of the newspapers of the celebrations in New York City. Nora enjoyed the resurgence in her social life and took full advantage of the return of young men to go on many dates. Nora also leveraged her position in the employment office to accept various government positions in places such as Washington, D.C., and New York. While employed in New York State in 1949, four years after the war ended, Nora met a young former air force pilot and mechanic named Daniel Mulholland. He proposed on their first date, and while it took her a while to accept his proposal, the two married and settled in Pittsburgh's East End to raise a family.

*Part II*

# *Military Narratives*

# A B-24 Gunner's Survival in Enemy Territory

*Alex Antanovich Jr.,*

*As told to David Scott Beveridge*

Alex Antanovich Jr. was fortunate to safely return to his hometown of Cokeburg in Washington County, Pennsylvania, after serving in Europe during World War II. Antanovich parachuted to safety before his B-24 bomber crashed in Germany on a mission to cripple Nazi supply lines.

Allied air assaults over France and Germany during World War II were seeing their greatest successes in the spring of 1944. The daylight bombing raids were targeting strategic German-held railroads to cut off enemy supply lines, while others were pounding the French coast to drive back enemy forces. Nearly one thousand heavy bombers were flying missions that were also aimed at airfields and chemical and fuel stations. The B-24 Liberator, affectionately named LONI and carrying a crew of nine, did not fare so well. It crashed on May 30, 1944, near Rheine, Germany, after three of its four engines failed and the entire crew had bailed from the plane. Eight crew members were captured and held by the Nazis as prisoners of war. Incredibly, U.S. Army Air Force Sergeant Alex Antanovich Jr. evaded capture. Despite landing in enemy territory, he would be led by civilians to members of the resistance movement in Holland, where he was fed, clothed and sheltered for the next ten months. "I was in constant fear," said Antanovich, recalling his story that had all the makings of a suspenseful war novel.

His plane had taken off that day at 6:53 a.m. from Mendlesham, England, carrying fifteen 500-pound bombs. Thus the weight of the payload alone was 7,500 pounds. More than eighteen thousand B-24s, their wingspans spreading 110 feet wide, had been produced in Detroit, Michigan, by Consolidated Aircraft Corporation for the war effort. This company created the largest air fleet of its kind at the time. Antanovich, who was then twenty-one years old, had been trained to fire all of the plane's ten machine guns. World War II bombing crews faced some of the worst dangers in combat. "They were shooting at us," he says, while discussing his military experiences when he was eighty-two years old. "You could lose your life on takeoff. You're loaded down to capacity. There's no place to hide."

Antanovich received his training at Blythe Army Air Base in California. His crew used LONI to fly to England, following a route over Florida, South America, Africa and finally to Great Britain. Because the crew members all hailed from different ethnic backgrounds, they called themselves the League of Nations, Incorporated, and gave the plane the acronym LONI as its name. Antanovich entertained himself on the flights to England by watching the lights in the cities at night. "I was going to fight a war," he said. Little else was on his mind.

Antanovich had only been in England for a month and had flown four previous missions to Germany when his plane crashed. It dipped from formation with two of its engines smoking and one out of commission prior to reaching its intended target. Other members of the Thirty-fourth Bombing Group flying in nearby planes then lost sight of LONI, and no one reported seeing any parachutes. The sixty-six-foot-long plane's legacy was cut short before an artist had time to paint its name on its side, as was customary during the war.

"When the pilot said to bail out, I was in the tail of the plane," Antanovich says. "The pilot said to throw stuff out to lighten the load. A short time later, the tail gunner who stayed on the intercom said, 'Bail out,' and away he went." Antanovich was afraid to jump from the plane, having never done so before during his military training. "Why jump if you may never have to?" he thought. Being the last one left in the tail of the plane, Antanovich looked over the bomb bay to see what the pilot and co-pilot were doing, hoping they were regaining control of the aircraft. The co-pilot was readying for his jump, and Antanovich knew he had no choice but to do the same thing. "I went to the Lord," says Antanovich, who believed in God but was not an especially religious man at the time.

"I asked the Lord for help. I got a warm feeling over my body. I walked right over to that escape hatch and away I went. I lost my fear."

Over the course of the next several days, nearly everything Antanovich did went against what he was taught to do in the event that he became missing in action. When he regained his bearings on the ground, he realized he was separated from his crew. He had been told to run in such a situation and to keep on the move for twenty-four hours. "I went deeper into the woods and covered my parachute and started running," he said. He came upon a house and went in another direction, only to spot another. At that point, he went into the thicket and decided to attempt sleep. "I thought, 'Where am I going to run to?' If I kept running, I could have gotten killed." Several hours later, he awoke to the sound of a boy pumping water and decided to start walking again. Antanovich found himself back where he had hit the ground. He made the right move because he stumbled upon a friendly stranger while walking across a bicycle path. He whistled to get the man's attention, asking him in French if he spoke that language. The man shook his head no. Antanovich then asked him if he spoke English, and again, the man shook his head no. Antanovich pulled out a pocketbook that was part of his survival kit and designed to translate English phrases into the German language. He used it to inform the stranger that he was hungry and, in exchange, was given a handful of sugar. He also learned he was near Rheine, Germany, after showing the stranger one of the maps from the gear he carried. He was forty miles west of his B-24's target and twenty miles east of Germany's border with Holland. "I said, 'I'm American,'" Antanovich recalls. The stranger, who turned out to be a Prussian, flapped his arms in the air as a signal that he understood Antanovich was an airman. The man then pointed Antanovich in the direction of Holland, which was still in German hands. Antanovich set his compass and walked the remainder of the day and into the night. Tired and weary, he decided to make a bed of pine needles under a tall evergreen tree, where he slept his first night in Germany.

Antanovich was unarmed. In England, he had heard rumors that German troops were killing American soldiers on sight rather than taking prisoners because the Germans barely had enough supplies to care for their own soldiers. He had no idea just how much danger he was facing on his first full day in enemy territory. That same day, one of Hitler's shadow men, the Reichsleiter Martin Bormann, approved criminal combat methods under a German lynch law. By doing so, Bormann gave his seal of approval to mob justice, instructing German civilians to kill any Allied soldiers they encountered.

The next morning, Antanovich came upon railroad tracks and decided to follow them toward Holland. That could have been a mistake because German soldiers were guarding the rail lines. Upon spotting a man in the distance, he ducked for cover in the woods. That was when he stumbled upon a man and woman milking cows, a couple who helped him to reach safer quarters. "I said I was an American and I was hungry," he says. The couple gave him a sandwich, his only food in two days. They took him to a house and introduced him to an English-speaking woman. "She said, 'I know a man who knows a man who knows where to find the underground.'" The woman made a telephone call before escorting him by bicycle to a crossroads to meet another contact. "She said she didn't want to see him or for him to see her." This was designed to protect the identity of her contact, thus preventing the Nazis from unraveling the underground network through torture or other means.

Among other things, Antanovich's U.S. Army survival kit contained silk maps of Holland, France, Spain and Belgium, as well as three cigarettes. At his base in England, he had been advised to hold onto his belongings. But instead, he gave everything away to those who helped him along his way, except the maps of Holland and Belgium. "Anything I had that they asked for, I gave to them," Antanovich says. "I had a full pack of Camels. They told us not to smoke American tobacco because it was sweeter smelling and [the enemy would] recognize it." He even shed his army air force uniform for civilian clothes as a disguise after reaching the underground. That was a dangerous thing to do. Antanovich would be treated as a spy if he were caught, but he thought his chances were better in civilian clothes. He guessed that he would be even more noticeable in uniform and, if captured, he would be shot whether in uniform or not.

Antanovich's journey eventually took him to the home of Otto and Elisabeth Montagne on the outskirts of Hengelo, Holland. They were among many anti-Nazi couples in that area who secretly shielded Allied soldiers who had become separated from their units. Their visitors usually stayed in their home for three or four days until plans were made to return them to England, via France, Spain and Portugal. Spain temporarily held such MIAs as illegal immigrants before sending them to Portugal and from there to England, Antanovich was told. That escape route, however, was closed after Allied forces stormed Normandy, beginning June 6, 1944.

Antanovich's parents, Alex and Mary, received word on June 16, 1944, from the War Department that their son was missing in action. They were devastated. His younger brother John was then part of an army air force B-17 flight crew serving in the United States. While his family dealt with the news, Antanovich was being hidden in sixteen different houses, some for a few hours and others for a month or two. He found himself sandwiched under trapdoors on some occasions when German troops searched from house to house, looking for railroad workers to help them reopen supply routes. The Montagnes shared their home with him and three other soldiers for seven months. Mrs. Montagne provided them with clothing from a nearby textile factory, giving them identical dark blue shirts with vertical stripes to identify them to others involved in the resistance. The men even wore wooden shoes and distinguishing hairstyles and mustaches to appear as local residents.

Mrs. Montagne often walked with a cart great distances to gather enough food to feed her guests. Food was being rationed, and each house was permitted to use electric lights for only one hour a day. Two rabbits from the barn provided Christmas dinner, a meal that also included cheese, crackers and pudding. Antanovich and his companions lived out their long days in boredom either reading, holding conversations or learning to speak Dutch. They sometimes occupied their time by playing games of Battleship, using scraps of numbered paper as game pieces, or singing songs around a piano.

By March 1945, the Dutch liberation effort began to intensify. Resistance fighters ambushed Nazi General Hans Ratter on March 6, 1945. More than one hundred Dutchmen were killed in retaliation two days later. Antanovich spent that month hiding in a hut in the woods with an armed member of the Canadian Royal Air Force. Hitler's army was under attack on all fronts. "You could hear the gunfire getting close," Antanovich says. By the end of the month, Allied forces were racing across collapsing German defenses. On April 1, 1945, they had German troops surrounded in the Ruhr basin, while British troops rolled into Hengelo that same day. Antanovich was rescued by members of the Welsh Guard after walking arm in arm to freedom with a young Dutch woman. He could hardly believe it was actually happening after ten months of evading capture. He was taken to the guard's headquarters in Brussels before being sent to a U.S. military facility in Paris, France. "I had no identification," Antanovich says. He was later returned to England to be identified by members of his bombing group, only to find all of his possessions gone. To his relief, he was told the other members of his aircrew had survived German prisoner of war camps. On April 24, 1945, his mother was told by the military that he was returned to active duty and was being rotated back to the United States. Antanovich did not say whether his family had given him up for lost, but their relief at the news of his rescue was boundless. They were one of the lucky families whose son returned alive and unhurt.

Following the war, Antanovich went home to rural Washington County and married the former Betty Porter. The couple had two sons,

Workers at a Pittsburgh mill celebrate V-E Day by making the "V for Victory" sign made famous by Winston Churchill. *William J. Gaughan Collection, University of Pittsburgh.*

Over 400,000 Americans gave their lives in World War II. The city of Pittsburgh mourned its losses at a 1945 Memorial Day exercise in Calvary Cemetery. A statue of a Civil War soldier presides over the scene, commemorating losses from that war. *Carnegie Library of Pittsburgh.*

Alex and David, who died in childhood, and a daughter, Yvonne. He worked as a coal miner in Beth-Energy Corporation's Cokeburg Mine, from which he retired in 1985 after working in the coal fields for twenty-four years. He says it was amazing to be part of such a great generation, one that witnessed serious hardships and major triumphs. "The men of today will never compete with what we went through," he said. "We went through the Great Depression. We saw the TV come in. When I was a kid, farmers were working with horses. The doctor would come in a horse and buggy."

Antanovich also began attending church after returning home from the war. One day while reading the Bible, he came upon a verse in Psalms that states, "I sought the Lord, and he heard me, and delivered me from all my fears."

# The Integrity of a Soldier

*Charles Bates,*

*As told to Stephanie J. Fetsko*

Born in 1916 in the Lawrenceville section of Pittsburgh, Charles Bates was the son of a steel construction worker. He was one of thirteen children, of whom seven died in infancy or early childhood. "Today my parents would have been investigated by Allegheny County Child and Youth Services, but that didn't happen back then," Charlie says. When he was five, his Irish Catholic parents moved the family to the predominantly German working-class suburb of Millvale, just across the Allegheny River from Pittsburgh. Charlie quit high school to help his family after his sophomore year. He was glad that he learned how to type in high school, as it was a skill that served him well for a lifetime career in the military.

Charlie knew he wanted to be a soldier even at the young age of fourteen. He did not pick a particularly propitious time to quit school. "It was 1932, and we were at the bottom of the Depression," he says. Two years later, he entered the New Deal's Civilian Conservation Corps. Charlie loved it. "The CCC was a lot like the army," he recalls joyously. "You lived forty-four men to a barracks, two hundred to a camp. A potbellied stove was our only heat. We fell out for reveille early and raised the American flag." Like every other young man in the CCC, Bates earned a dollar a day.

"We had to send twenty-five dollars home every month," he says. "We got to keep five dollars. I saved my money. I worked at a camp on Tussey Mountain in Centre County, Pennsylvania, making firebreaks by hand with a rake, clearing brush." At times they were even shot at by careless hunters and they had to hit the ground. Charlie says that the year he served in the CCC was his transition from a boy to a man.

Upon his discharge from the CCC, Bates got a job at McCann's in downtown Pittsburgh working as a warehouseman. He tried to enlist in the army in early 1941, but they refused him due to his bad teeth. Then, on December 7, 1941, Japan bombed Pearl Harbor. The United States was at war, and everything changed.

On January 12, 1942, only a month and five days after Pearl Harbor, Charlie joined the U.S. Army Air Corps. He was twenty-five years old. The army accepted him on waivers due to his dental problems, which were later corrected by an army dentist. He entered the military as a buck private, just like nearly every other guy entering the service.

Charlie was sent to Kessler Army Air Corps Base in Biloxi, Mississippi, for six weeks of indoctrination and training. "It was strict, but far from the rigorous training you often hear about," he says. On February 26, 1942, Charlie and his fellow inductees embarked on a troop ship, the USS *Haan*, with no knowledge of their destination. They left the port of New Orleans and sailed into the Gulf of Mexico, which Charlie says was "infested with enemy submarines." They proceeded through the famed engineering marvel, the Panama Canal, that Charlie had read about as a child.

His assignment as an aviation gasoline supply technician was to maintain the transfer of high-octane gasoline from oceangoing tankers from the Balboa docks to a jungle tank storage area approximately ten miles from the docks. Planes, ships, barges and other military forms of transportation utilized this fuel. In Panama, he was under an American civilian engineer, Mr. Lewis, whom Charlie describes as the "meanest man in the world" but who, oddly, "liked me." Lewis said, "I want a man with stripes," and in a year, Charlie had three stripes as a sergeant. Mr. Lewis invited Charlie to his home in Panama City. There he demonstrated his short temper and meanness by knocking his plate of fried eggs to the floor, complaining to his wife that he didn't like the edges fried crisp. Lewis was on the phone once when lightning struck the line. The lightning knocked him down.

He was so hated that one of Charlie's fellow GIs asked, "Shall we call the ambulance for the SOB?" They did, and Lewis recovered.

There were about seventeen civilian Panamanian workers and one soldier who assisted Charlie in moving the gasoline. As they emptied the gasoline tanks, they replaced the gasoline with water to prevent explosion under the hot tropical sun. They had no mishaps. Since Charlie worked in a land of foreigners, he quickly learned some working Spanish words. He at least learned enough words to keep the fuel from blowing up or catching fire with the phrases "no fumar aqui" (no smoking here) and "muy peligroso" (very dangerous). Once in 1943, Charlie and his Panamanian crew were unloading a British tanker in the canal when a U.S. Marine demanded an ID from a British sailor. The drunken sailor, returning to his ship, said, "Go f--- yourself!" The marine shot him once in the stomach. Bates yelled to his Panamanian crew, "Abajo!" and

Only four days after Pearl Harbor, Pittsburghers in large numbers stopped at these war bond booths on Oliver Avenue at Smithfield Street, unmindful of the snowfall. *Carnegie Public Library.*

everybody hit the ground. Charlie was afraid the marine would spray the entire group with bullets.

Loneliness and despondency took a surprising toll. A number of young soldiers committed suicide, a fact that was not publicized for fear of further demoralization. One barracks had so many suicides that it was even referred to as the "suicide barracks." Even in his own barracks, Charlie awoke one night to the sound of a fellow soldier struggling to hold a rifle butt between his feet while aiming the muzzle at his head. Realizing that the solider was distraught over a recently received "Dear John" letter and intent on suicide with Charlie's weapon, Charlie shouted at him, "Not with my gun, you don't!" The reprimand was enough to jolt the soldier to his senses and save his life.

Charlie and the other soldiers went into Panama City on leave to go dancing. His officers ordered them to be careful about disclosing information to the girls with whom they spent their time for fear of German spies who were willing to pay for information. Charlie wonders how well the men took heed of this warning, especially under the influence of alcohol. "The soldiers were not at all careful," he says. "Venereal disease was so widespread that they had a doctor inspect us. It was always a surprise visit." The doctor came about every two or three months, often in the middle of the night. The GIs crudely called it a "short-arm inspection." Soldiers went to Coconut Grove, a prostitution district. The potential for violence was incredible. Once a soldier had been returned to the base for fighting in Panama City and was incarcerated in the guardhouse. Prisoners were permitted exercise under armed guard, but when "the prisoner was giving him a hard time, the guard shot him right in the head," Charlie relates. He did not witness the incident, but word of it quickly traveled across the base. Charlie found this job in Panama interesting and exciting work but obtained great satisfaction and a sense of relief when his tour of duty was completed. Charlie served twenty-eight months there.

On July 4, 1944, Charlie returned to the United States. He was sent to the Aviation Battalion at Geiger Air Corps Base in Spokane, Washington, for a short tour of duty until his transfer request came through for Hamilton Army Air Corps Base near San Raphael, California. In 1945, his work involved being an airplane flight dispatcher at Hammer Army Air Corps Base in Fresno, California. In an interesting story, one of the staff sergeants

Sergeant Charles Bates, U.S. Army Air Corps. *Charles Bates.*

had a hot date. He was the engineer on a flight to San Francisco and talked Charlie into taking over for him. He told Charlie, "There's nothing to it. You just watch the altimeter and the cylinder head temperature and a few other dials." The flight arrived without incident, but the colonel wrote in his report, "Next time send me an engineer who knows what he's doing."

Since the war was coming to an end and many air bases were starting to close down, the army needed to supply logistical personnel to aid in handling the closures. The military assigned Bates, along with ten soldiers who had no prior experience in this capacity and were waiting to be discharged from the service, to close the bases. He was able to train them to accomplish the assignment with precision and accuracy. In addition, his role was to assist in closing the hospital's eight surgical operating units.

After the war ended in August 1945, Charlie, still haunted by his memories of the Great Depression, decided to make the military his career. He volunteered for the U.S. occupation of Japan. His Japanese tour was from March 1947 to September 1948. During this time, Charlie was promoted to staff sergeant, serving as warehouse supervisor while with the 591st Air Material Squadron, Ashiya Air Base, Japan. He worked

The August 15, 1945 issue of the *Pittsburgh Post-Gazette* announced the end of the war. Cartoonist Cy Hungerford held out the prospect for a world without war. *Carnegie Library of Pittsburgh.*

in logistics, keeping track of inventory and ordering parts. It was a very pleasant and interesting experience to learn the culture of the Far East. He had a very unusual meeting with some people who were in Japan when Hiroshima was bombed. He says that it was a pleasure to speak with a German priest and several groups of Catholic nuns from Ireland, England, France and Germany who aided the elderly people left to die in the streets of Kokura, Japan. He recalls a happy memory of a time when his unit had some surplus nylon parachutes that were to be destroyed. When the nuns who worked at one of the orphanages became aware of this, they asked if they could use this material for making clothing. So he donated the parachutes. Later, Charlie learned that the nuns had made beautiful First Holy Communion dresses for the Japanese children.

Once back in the United States, Bates took advantage of every educational opportunity to which he was entitled that he believed would advance his military career. His military courses included personnel management; redistribution and marketing; equipment cooling specialist; refrigeration and air conditioning specialist; and automotive and diesel repairman. After serving assignments as close to home as the Pittsburgh airport in Coraopolis and as remote as Grand Forks, North Dakota, Master Sergeant Charles Bates retired from the 464 3rd Support Squadron, Semi-Automatic Ground Environment, on May 30, 1962. He was ready to head back home to Pittsburgh. Charlie became a civilian and received his retirement orders from the armed forces after service of twenty years, four months and eleven days.

When Charlie served as a disposal agent at the Greater Pittsburgh Airport Air Reserve Center in Pittsburgh in 1985, a Pittsburgh newspaper interviewed him regarding a mysterious phone call he received while working at the center. This call concerned the B-25 bomber that had crashed into the Monongahela River. This plane had been an inventoried item that was sold. The mysterious caller inquired whether he could purchase parts of a similar plane, making it appear as though the plane had been found. Bates informed the caller that he would have to contact the plane's owner. When the caller was asked for his name, he ended the call. The mystery of the B-25 bomber, known as the Ghost Bomber of the Monongahela, began on January 31, 1956, and continues to this day.

In civilian life, Charlie remains active in the Veterans of Foreign Wars (VFW). He helped his community preserve a World War II monument in a park near his home. A very interesting person who has a very positive attitude about his life and career as a soldier, Bates loved the military and has no regrets about participating in a part of history that will never be forgotten. He is proud to have served his country and would do it again. He feels that the United States' involvement in World War II was a necessity that helped regain peace and balance in the world. His other great love was his wife, Mary, to whom he was married in 1948. They were married for fifty-six years. Charlie described her as a very compassionate and loving person, and it was not until after her death that he found that she had kept every letter he had written to her while he was overseas in the service. Charlie thought the world of Mary and deeply appreciated her loving devotion and her support of his military career.

# WHEELING AND DEALING

*Sidney Bernstein,*

*As told to Rocco Ross*

S id Bernstein was born in the Oakland neighborhood of Pittsburgh, Pennsylvania. A very social and mischievous youngster, Sid spent much of his free time on the streets of the Uptown Pittsburgh neighborhood near Duquesne University. Because he looked older than he actually was, Sid was able to get into bars and clubs when he was only sixteen years old. He met all types of people and new friends in this adult environment and was having too much fun to really pay any serious attention to the great war erupting in Europe.

Bernstein never even considered joining the armed forces. He remembers that before World War II, soldiers had a negative connotation. He thought that they were viewed mostly as bums because many poor and uneducated men who could not find a civilian job would join the army just to be able to eat and earn a little bit of money. Sid also felt no call to arms as a sense of service because he, like most people of his time, did not want to get involved in the conflict across the Atlantic.

His cavalier lifestyle, along with his negative impression of soldiers, changed completely after the bombing of Pearl Harbor in December 1941. In 1942, Sid was drafted into the United States Army. A large meeting was held for the newly drafted men at Taylor Allderdice High School. Reluctant, but required to attend, Bernstein showed up to find that preliminary medical screening and interviewing were already underway. Anyone who was obviously not physically suited for the army had a black X marked on his hand. Bernstein pleaded with the examiners to be given an X, but he was unsuccessful.

After being sworn into the service, Sid was sent by train to St. Petersburg, Florida. From there he made further training stops in Chanute Field, Illinois, and Long Island, New York. Finally, he was sent to a base near the coast of Maine. When Sid arrived in Maine and reported to his outfit, he discovered that they were to be sent overseas immediately. Having talked only with other low-ranking soldiers and no officers, Bernstein inquired about joining another unit that was not leaving so soon. A soldier told Sid that there was another unit stationed not far away, so he took off to find a more suitable group. The fact that he was able to undertake such a change without official orders attests to the lack of organization in those early days of the war. The newly minted word "SNAFU" (*Situation Normal, All F---ed Up*—or alternately *Fouled Up*), describing the muddled state of military organization, in this case, worked to Sid's advantage.

When Bernstein arrived at the other unit, it was nightfall, so he found a covered truck in which he slept that night. The next morning he recalls being pulled out of the truck by his legs and questioned by officers about his identity and where he had come from. Bernstein told the officers that he was instructed to join this unit and that when he arrived, he did not want to wake anyone up, so he slept in the truck. With that flimsy explanation and no transfer papers, Sid Bernstein became the newest member of a combat engineer unit.

The same amiable personality that had allowed Sid to attract friends and women in the bars at home would soon allow him to gain the friendship and trust of the men and officers in his military unit. Sid was placed in the motor pool, where he was assigned to drive a jeep for a captain. One of his "missions" was to drive the captain to visit his girlfriend. Sid was instructed to drop him off at the town where she worked and to pick him up two days later. In return for his quiet cooperation, Bernstein was given two days' personal leave. He quickly learned that in the military, keeping one's mouth shut was usually advantageous.

Another job that made Bernstein popular among his fellow soldiers was his role as alcohol transporter. Alcohol was difficult to come by at the Maine base. The officers would send Sid to nearby towns to purchase beer and liquor for them. As a token of their appreciation, they would often give him some for himself. While he was at these towns, Sid would be sure to buy some alcohol for the other enlisted men in his unit.

Before long, Sid and his group were sent out on a ship bound for the South Pacific. He remembers the time on ship being tough because "you did not know exactly where you were going or what you would have to do when you got there." When they arrived in the South Pacific, Sid's group of combat engineers typically followed marines onto the islands and began clearing the beaches so that tanks and other armored vehicles could make their way on land. Once the area was secure, the engineers sometimes began building airstrips to allow planes to take off and land on the beach.

Such missions were not as trouble-free as they might sound. During his time on the islands, Sid recalls a lot of fighting. He remembers seeing fallen marines as they stormed the beaches of the islands. The Japanese were ferocious fighters and would entrench themselves in the tiny islands. On one particular island, Bernstein recalls that taking over the beach for an airstrip was the only objective. The marines drove the Japanese into the jungle, but they were not required to go in after them because taking over the entire island was deemed unnecessary. One day, a force of Australian soldiers came to the island and said they were going in after the Japanese. Bernstein and his friends wished them luck but knew they would probably be slaughtered. To their astonishment, Sid found that "the Australians turned out to be even more merciless fighters than the Japanese." Before long, they returned to report that the island was free of any Japanese presence. Because of that, Bernstein gained the utmost respect for his Australian allies.

As Bernstein traveled through the South Pacific, he faced death several times. Sailing between islands, he remembers Japanese fighter planes strafing the boats and kamikaze pilots dive-bombing in an attempt to sink the ship he was on. As U.S. forces drove nearer to Japan, the fighting grew more intense. When Bernstein finally made his way to Okinawa, he saw death and destruction everywhere. The memories of that horror would never leave him. Stacks of marines' bodies, five and six feet tall, lay all around.

The suffering and death of fellow Americans took its psychological toll on Bernstein and his buddies. On several of the islands that the combat engineers worked, they encountered liberated POWs. These men had been beaten and starved by the Japanese. "It was," Sid says, "beyond belief." Those images, coupled with the sight of mounds of fallen marines, caused many soldiers to lose all inhibitions in battle. Bernstein remembers that it was commonplace for Americans to shoot surrendering Japanese in retaliation for their treatment of Americans. Such was the face of war.

As chaotic and disastrous as the war was at times, Sid experienced many entertaining and jaunty situations. For example, once on an island in the South Pacific, food, water and other supplies were being delivered in bulk to a designated location before being divided and rerouted to the soldiers around the island. When the goods would get to Sid's group, he and the other men always felt as if they were being shortchanged. Being a confident smooth-talker, Bernstein took some friends and a company truck on a mission to the depot where the supplies were being shipped. Once they arrived, Sid distracted the soldiers who were working by talking to them about women, the news or anything else he could think of to hold their attention. While he was keeping these men busy, his friends were stealing food and other items and loading up the truck they had brought. The rest of their unit was delighted upon their return to camp.

Sid discovered that another effective way to cut through red tape and get additional luxuries and benefits was to become a military police officer. However, a soldier cannot simply change his assignment designation in the military. So Sid and some friends "acquired" MP helmets and armbands and went around the islands posing as MPs. Soldiers who were afraid of getting in trouble would bribe them with money and other goods.

American soldiers were not the only victims of Sid's schemes. He once encountered a Swiss paratrooper who had a pocketful of money. Sid and his pals convinced the Swiss soldier that they had connections that could get him all types of food and alcohol. The condition was that he had to pay up front. After handing over $300, the paratrooper never saw Sid and his buddies again.

When Bernstein was not scamming on the islands, he was fraternizing with Hollywood stars. One of the highlights of his time in the South Pacific was meeting actor Lew Ayers. Sid recognized Ayers in the Philippines, where he was working as a medic. Ayers had become famous for his part in the 1930 war movie *All Quiet on the Western Front* and the *Young Doctor Kildare* movie series. He had attempted to join the Medical

Corps but was refused because of their inability to protect such a famous personage. He then declared himself a conscientious objector, resulting in a change in their decision and his acceptance as a medic. Ayers served with distinction in the Pacific Theater and New Guinea. The two spent time together talking about Ayers's career and both of their experiences in the war.

Bernstein recalls the end of the war, when the United States dropped the atomic bombs on Hiroshima and Nagasaki. Although not part of an attacking force, Bernstein's combat engineers would have more than likely been involved in a land invasion of Japan had that option been exercised. Bernstein views the use of the atomic bombs as "a good decision by President Truman" because it saved so many American lives.

When the war ended, Bernstein was discharged from the army but decided that he wanted to continue working with the armed forces. Sid

In 1945, Pittsburghers dedicated the downtown honor roll at Sixth and Forbes Avenues bearing the names of 1,021 residents of the First Ward who served in the nation's military. *Carnegie Library of Pittsburgh.*

joined the USO and worked for them for many years. It was not until after the war that Bernstein discovered the fate of European Jews in the Holocaust. As a Jewish man himself, Bernstein had a deep sympathy for the suffering of his fellow Jews.

Although he was reluctant to enter the army, Sid acknowledges that the military gave his life discipline and direction that he otherwise may never have gained. He looks back on his days of service with both fond and earnest memories. The war permitted Sid to make many new friends, travel the world and serve his country in a meaningful way at that crucial time in history.

# A Soldier's Brush
# with Death

*Raymond Book,*

*As told to Stephanie J. Fetsko*

A native of Pittsburgh's Mount Washington neighborhood, Raymond T. Book was only nineteen years of age when he enlisted in the army on April 15, 1943. He was shipped to Ireland for basic training. There he became skilled in weaponry and was taught to put a machine gun together blindfolded. After basic training, he was sent to England and was assigned to the Fourth Army Division. Departing from England, he boarded a ship that took him to one of the most memorable days in history—D-Day. He served in the First Army, commanded by General George Patton.

On that infamous day, June 6, 1944, Book nervously waited on board ship with thousands of other young men to storm the beaches of Normandy, France. He recalls that his battalion was scheduled to land on Omaha Beach a day or two after the initial landing. As he was climbing down the rope ladder from the LST (landing ship tank) to the landing craft, his hand slipped, causing him to lose his grasp of the rope and fall into the icy waters. With all his gear and a tripod for a 105-caliber machine gun strapped to his back, he sank like a lead weight. He miraculously survived the incident when a fellow soldier quickly pulled him out of the frigid waters. Book narrowly escaped from death—not just from drowning, but also from being crushed between the ship and the LST rocking together in the choppy waters. They bumped against

LSTs (landing ship tanks) used on the D-Day invasion were manufactured by Dravo Corporation at the Neville Island Works in the Ohio River, just downstream from Pittsburgh. Evident in front is the bay door, which swung downward, forming a ramp to unload amphibious landing craft, tanks and other vehicles. *Senator John Heinz History Center.*

each other while the men climbed from the ship to the landing craft. His soaked clothing did not excuse him; like everyone else, he had to plunge straight ahead. There was no turning back. In fact, there was no change of clothing for another month or two.

Upon landing on Omaha Beach just after the first day of the D-Day invasion, Book's platoon saw bodies of many fallen comrades. There was still fighting to do before the beachhead was secured. Although the worst of the battle had been fought, they still had to face sporadic German fire. The howitzers already set up on the beach from the previous day were manned until they were knocked out by the enemy. As the platoon moved from the beachhead, they would be left to fight their way across France without artillery pieces for a long time before the howitzers could be replaced. Book and his battalion then continued on a northwestern route

"Back the attack" was a common theme in several of the war bond drives. Dramatic battlefield scenes helped connect those on the homefront with the nation's military effort. *William J. Gaughan Collection, University of Pittsburgh.*

to Cherbourg, France, where they were assigned to assist in the liberation from German occupation. As they made their way, they encountered little resistance. The American infantry had passed through the previous day, gaining some control over the territory, but they still faced some shelling from the Germans.

Book recalls fighting German forces in the liberation of several small French villages, as well as Le Havre in France, Bastogne in Belgium and Hamburg in Germany. Because he was one of the few who had a driver's license, he was able to drive a truck for some of this distance. Trucks were not always available, however, and he estimates that he traveled about half the distance on foot. In December 1944, the Allies encountered a lot of resistance from the Germans around the town of Bastogne. The Germans had broken through the Allied lines, surrounded the city and demanded its surrender. U.S. General McAuliffe gave his famous reply to the German ultimatum: "Nuts!" McAuliffe was noted for his lack of profanity. Book and his buddies endured the siege, consisting mostly of artillery shells. No waves of German soldiers appeared. At last they were saved when Patton's Third Army broke through and liberated the city two days after Christmas. It was only after the siege was broken that Book and his buddies realized how precarious their position had been. The fighting around Bastogne was part of a campaign known to history as the Battle of the Bulge. The winter he endured, 1944–45, was an extremely cold one. Book suffered frostbite on his toes, but he says that his condition was only minor compared to other men in his platoon who suffered severe frostbite and other serious injuries.

Book's biggest battle against the German resistance took place in the city of Cologne. He recalls that the city was leveled and that he had dug in to fire his machine gun. The worst of the fighting had occurred the day before he arrived, leaving dead bodies of German soldiers in the houses and a multitude of dead animals, primarily cows and horses, lying in the streets.

There were many times Book and the other soldiers would go for days without food because the supply tents were blown up. However, the men were provided with K-rations that included bouillon cubes, which mixed easily in hot water and became broth. And there were always chocolate bars to provide quick energy. There were no regular supply deliveries and no hot meals. Trucks would drop supplies along the road to be distributed

Recruits from Pittsburgh are shown how to fire a forty-millimeter gun at ground targets. *Carnegie Library of Pittsburgh.*

as the soldiers passed. They slept on the ground. There were intervals when he couldn't even remember when he last had a shower.

While in one unknown town, Book recalls talking to another soldier when his sergeant told him to pick up a sack that was lying on the opposite side of the street. Book did not hear the sergeant's order, so another soldier said that he would go get the sack. As the soldier went over to pick up the sack, he stepped on a land mine hidden under a paving stone, killing him instantly. Book remembers just how lucky he was that day and how saddened he was that it came at the price of another soldier's life.

Another encounter with the Germans occurred while he was walking through the roads in France. Along these roads grew what is known as a hedgerow, an eight- to ten-foot-high barrier of bushy shrubs that lined the rural roads. While walking through the countryside, he and about ten other soldiers heard a noise. When they looked through the hedgerow, they saw about fifty to sixty German soldiers all marching in the opposite direction directly on the other side of the same hedgerow. Book says that they "were a noisy bunch" and that he and his comrades continued walking silently, knowing that they would not be heard over the noise being made by the Germans.

Toward the end of the war, Book kept guard at the infamous German concentration camp Auschwitz after its liberation. At Auschwitz, he saw dead bodies lying all around the grounds. Bodies were stacked up four by four like railroad ties. In one of these piles, Book saw a foot move and reported it to his captain. The person was pulled from the pile and was provided medical attention. Book does not know whether the person survived. He saw this person and several others barely existing, weighing about eighty undernourished pounds of "nothing but skin and bones." He saved photos of three corpses. The horrible mutilation of thousands of innocent victims was an unforgettable atrocity.

Throughout Book's military career, he was only able to get a glance at General Eisenhower from afar but was able to see General Marshall and General Patton close up. He says that Patton was a real character, a showpiece, and that everything about his appearance, down to his pearl-handled holster guns, was highly polished.

Book says that the war was necessary. "We needed to put the Germans in their place and to straighten out the world." He recalls that, in all the

To raise morale on the homefront, trophies of war, including this captured German tank, minus its track, were shipped back to Pittsburgh, where they were placed on display. *William J. Gaughan Collection, University of Pittsburgh.*

places he had been, his fellow comrades were always optimistic and their morale was high.

Book was awarded four battle stars and four bronze stars. He is also in the process of filling out papers for a Purple Heart, since he was injured from a shell that landed ten yards from a jeep in which he was a passenger. Again, he was lucky to have suffered only superficial wounds to his eye. He finished his military career as a soldier with the Eighth Division and was honorably discharged at the end of the war.

Raymond Book went on to be elected a Pennsylvania state representative (1982–90), serving four terms. In 1985, he succeeded in getting his most notable bill passed in the Pennsylvania House. It made it possible for organ donors to be identified on driver's licenses. His bill also allowed the hospitals to ask the deceased person's family if they could use vital organs to help sustain life for others. Book, who had witnessed so many deaths during the war, is most proud of a bill intended to save lives.

# WHERE THE HELL IS PEARL HARBOR?

*Bill Gruber,*

*As told to Sandy Doyle*

Bill Gruber grew up in Oakland, the oldest of four boys. At Central Catholic High School, he was on both the swim team and the football team. Bill remembers that before World War II, residents of Oakland took the bus or streetcar to work, as few people had cars. There was so little traffic that they would rope off the streets for winter sled riders, putting burnt coal and ashes at the bottom of the hills so the sleds could stop in case a car did come along.

Bill recalls that many people in his neighborhood were isolationists before the war. On December 7, 1941, he was helping his father wallpaper the dining room when a neighbor came to tell them about the Japanese attack at Pearl Harbor. Bill's dad said, "Where the hell is Pearl Harbor?" The American people learned a lot more about Pearl Harbor the following day when President Roosevelt asked Congress to declare war. Suddenly in his neighborhood, isolationist talk vanished as the country mobilized for war. Bill had high school to finish. He had always "loafed with older guys," and after graduating from high school in 1942, he couldn't wait to turn eighteen and join his friends who were already serving in the military. Bill's dad was not thrilled about his son being in the service and told him that the war would be over soon. If he didn't have to go, why not wait until he was drafted by the army?

Because Bill had been on the swim team, he loved the thought of water and ships and wanted to enlist in the navy. Reluctantly, his parents signed the form so that he could join at seventeen. His uncles from World War I told him what to expect: "Average fellows were treated like kings when they were in uniform!"

Even though Bill thought that the United States was losing the war at the time, he was confident that the Allies would win the war eventually. England, France and Japan had bigger navies, but the U.S. Navy was building ships right here on the Ohio River and would catch up fast.

Bill feels that the military historically wanted young men because older men would actually think about the danger involved in what they were being ordered to do. According to Bill Gruber, "They don't want old guys who could think." The night he left Pittsburgh for basic training was his first time leaving the city. Security was tight because "loose lips sink ships." None of the men knew their destinations. A line of about two

The March 25, 1942 issue of the *Pittsburgh Post-Gazette* showed U.S. Marines giving new recruits the "send-off they deserve," accompanied by American Legion Drum and Bugle Corps, as they marched down Wood Street to the train station. *Carnegie Library of Pittsburgh.*

hundred marines and sailors who had enlisted and one hundred older army draftees was marched across the Smithfield Street Bridge in the dark to the P&LE station. The bridge closed down to one lane of traffic. Navy MPs and army SPs with side arms and leggings tried to keep away the civilians who had come to see the men off. Lots of civilians, including Bill's mother, his aunts and two or three girlfriends, were there. Bill's dad yelled, "Don't volunteer for anything and do what they tell you!"

The men were put on an antique steam train called back into service to convey troops to their secret basic training destinations. For security and safety reasons, all recruits were told to sit on the floor. When the packed train pulled out at midnight with full military honors, Bill whacked the seat above him with his hand and dust flew up from the long unused seat. It hadn't even been cleaned! Two hours later, the train stopped in the pitch black of the countryside. Pulling between two other trains for security, they transferred the army draftees to one train and the marines to another. The sixty navy recruits stayed on their original train. By 7:00 a.m., they were at Samson Naval Training Station, outside Ithaca, New York. Disembarking, Bill thought, "I'm in New York! This is New York dirt!" He observed units marching and thought, "I hope they don't think that I'm going to do that!"

Boot camp lasted fourteen weeks. Bill explains the derivation of the term "boot camp." It actually refers to the leggings worn by soldiers in previous wars. If you were a "boot" you had to wear leggings that snapped up the side of your leg over your boots. The officers could tell the "newbies" from the more seasoned recruits by their "boots" or leggings. One of the things that newbies had to do was navigate a one-mile obstacle course. Mud was made around the course with hoses. Bill was in good shape from playing football and easily completed the course. Even though rifles were not used in the navy, the recruits were taught to break down rifles and clean them. Bill had never fired a gun, but he proved to be a good shot, clustering them close to the bull's eye on the target range.

Bill had a seven-day leave before he was to report to the Brooklyn Navy Yard for his overseas deployment. His father, who was the head accountant at Pittsburgh Steel Company, now Wheeling-Pittsburgh Steel, took him to his office in the Grant Building to "show him off." Bill met about fifty employees. Pride had overcome his father's initial reluctance concerning his son's enlistment. There were three other Pittsburghers from his unit on leave here at the same time. Bill's mother realized that he could stay a day longer with them if he flew back to New York instead of taking the train with his fellow sailors. Bill decided to play a joke on his friends. He told them that he was going to go AWOL and would not return to the navy to go overseas. They were aghast, saying, "You're making a mistake! You're liable to get shot!" After his flight to New York, Bill took a cab from the airport to the barracks and got there before his friends. When they arrived at 1:00 a.m., they found him sleeping in his bunk.

Bill was sent to Providence, Rhode Island, for gunnery training. There the trainees lived in sheet metal Quonset huts. For two days they used a movie simulator. The object of the simulation was to shoot as fast as possible when an aircraft came on screen from any angle. On the first day, Bill shot down three planes. On the second day, the sky was darkened and clouds added, but he still shot down three planes. He "took to it."

Eight of the gunners were sent to Dam Neck, Virginia, about five miles from Virginia Beach. They had five days to get from Providence to Dam Neck carrying sealed orders in an envelope. Dam Neck was a small base run by a lieutenant wearing sandals with his shirttail out. With only about a dozen ships' companies permanently stationed there, to Bill it seemed like a resort. The men stationed there woke up to a recording of Glen Miller's band instead of reveille. They would go into Virginia Beach at night. Bill was there for six or eight weeks, training with huge guns embedded in concrete, pointing out to sea. Gunning was loud, but in those days they didn't have earplugs. When fired, the sound bouncing back could be felt throughout Bill's entire body. The commercial fishermen knew to stay away.

His sealed orders said that he was assigned to the USS *Phelps*, a small destroyer hunting German U-boats. Small destroyers were popularly called "tin cans" and held about 150 men. Bill had requested to be on an aircraft carrier and was transferred off the *Phelps*. Six weeks later, the *Phelps* was sunk and more than 100 sailors died.

Bill was sent to the brand-new aircraft carrier the USS *Franklin D. Roosevelt*, which was constructed at the Brooklyn Navy Yard. Christened the USS *Coral Sea* on April 29, 1945, the ship was renamed for the fallen president the following month. Bill has a card that says "original crew."

Mesta Machine Company produced a wide variety of guns for the war. In this photograph, which required two joined exposures to make a continuous picture, men pose atop one of the largest guns. *Senator John Heinz History Center.*

He is still amazed that with all of the security that went with moving troops to various locations, the German or Japanese spies never found them but the "bobby soxers" always did. The girls clustered around the train windows with gifts of cigarettes, candy and their addresses. Bill wrote to some of them. The *Roosevelt* held five thousand sailors and marines. As big as three football fields, it had fifty-four guns in the main battery. Gruber's mount was a ten-millimeter (five-inch) machine gun. The guns were numbered evenly on the starboard side and odd on the port side. Bill's gun was #3 on the port side. It had a range of twenty-two miles. Eight-inch and sixteen-inch guns could go even farther. Each gun had a crew of four men above and four men below the gun deck who delivered shells and powder. All eight learned to do each job required in loading. Shells were lined up around the bulkhead. They were put into a hoist, and then a powder keg was added to the shell. When loading the shells from below, if one did not close the hatch with the palm of the hand, with fingers out of the way, it was easy to lose a hand. Bill recalls seeing a shell come up with a dismembered hand on the top.

When in his anti-aircraft "open tub" gun mount, the gunner was strapped in a standing position so he could lean back and fire overhead. His feet were strapped into cleats while the turret spun in a circle. The big mounts had a manual control to change direction, but there was no time to do that in the heat of battle. In battle they used a "fire control man" to swing the turret in the direction of the firing. While engaging the enemy, it was possible for the fire control men to be crushed to death between turning gun mounts where there was not enough clearance, even though there were striped pennant warnings posted on the bulkhead in the space between the guns.

The worst things that Bill saw on the *Roosevelt* were not battle related. One day, Bill and an acquaintance decided to go up to the deck to watch planes make their "tail hook" landings. The tail hooks were four-inch-diameter cables stretched horizontally across the deck of the ship. These cables caught the tail of the plane when it was landing on the deck so it did not fall off the end of the landing strip and into the water. The two men stood in a pit below the landing deck while observing. Bill kept his cigarettes rolled up in his tee shirt sleeve, and when his pack fell out, he bent down to pick it up. Just as he did, one of the cables snapped and whipped around, beheading the sailor standing next to him. Bill's first instinct was to run up and grab the head by the hair and bring it back to replace it on the body. He remembers blood pumping from two streams in his neck. Bill believes that he saw life in the man's eyes for about ten or twelve seconds after the decapitation. A few days later, Bill had a dream where he was in a long tunnel, like Pittsburgh's Liberty Tunnels. There was a head rolling ahead of him in the tunnel. Bill thought, "That head is beating me! It's outdistancing me! I'm losing to it!" Once in a while he thinks about that kid and his parents getting the letter from the navy. Bill has memories of another grisly accident aboard the *Roosevelt*. Once, when general quarters was sounded summoning the men to their battle stations, a sailor on the flight deck was so excited to be running for his gun turret that he forgot to duck near a plane. He ran right into the turning propeller. Bill couldn't stop to help because he was running to his own gun, but he shouted for a medic. Nothing could be done for him. The memories of these tragic losses continue to haunt Bill.

Bill had a great deal of respect for his commanding officer, Lieutenant Rau, who had graduated from Annapolis. The lieutenant and his young bride (a runner-up for Miss New Jersey) had been featured in a Lux Soap advertisement showing Lieutenant Rau in uniform. One day while in the Brooklyn Navy Yard to resupply, a one-hundred-pound bomb was found to be defective on delivery. Lieutenant Rau asked Bill and some other men to take it out in the open on the flight deck. Lieutenant Rau and Bill

Gruber were going to defuse it. The men on the flight deck were moved to starboard. Lieutenant Rau had one pair of pliers, and Bill straddled the bomb with another pair of pliers. In the tense moments of defusing the bomb, a soldier named Holderad was singing a popular song: "Put your little foot, put your little foot, put your little foot right down…" Despite the distraction, they disabled the radio fuse successfully. While in port, the sailors were to be given liberty, which would be especially good for Holderad, who would be able to see his family in nearby Brooklyn. Lieutenant Rau took Holderad's liberty away for his thoughtlessness during such a suspenseful time.

When the war in Europe ended, the *Roosevelt* was too big to fit through the Panama Canal, so it sailed around South America to the Pacific. With the news of Hiroshima and Nagasaki, the men on his ship asked each other, "What's an atom bomb?" In all of that time at sea, the *Roosevelt* did not engage in a major battle. After Japan's defeat, those servicemen who had been in the military the longest and had been stationed overseas got more points toward discharge. Bill had enough points to get out but stayed an extra ninety days when Lieutenant Rau asked him to train new gunner recruits. After the tragic accidents he had witnessed, Bill always stressed safety.

Discharged in 1946, after returning to Pittsburgh, Bill couldn't help calling the wall the "bulkhead," the floor the "deck" and the stairway the "ladder." The city had a football draft for the pro teams of the Honus Wagner League that played baseball in the summer and football in the winter. Bill was drafted for the Oakland Rangers football team as a wide receiver. A first-round draft pick, he received fifteen dollars a game. The Rangers played at Sullivan Field in Oakland against teams from Aliquippa, McKees Rocks and Homewood.

Bill Gruber worked wherever he could make the most money. His day jobs changed through the years. He first worked at an A&P grocery store warehouse, then as a brakeman on the B&O Railroad out of Hazelwood and then making resins at Neville Chemical, where he became a member of the oil workers' union. He took the Pennsylvania State Troopers test and the civil service test and decided that he would work for whomever called him first. The North Side Post Office called first. Bill worked for the post office until his retirement in 1986. He is the only surviving brother in his family. Although he never married, he spends time with many nieces and nephews and their families in the area.

Bill observed firsthand the rise of the middle class when the returning GIs wanted change. Postwar America accomplished this with higher hourly wages, overtime pay and workers' compensation, resulting in a high standard of living for all. Because of the good wages, homeownership rose and more people were able to afford a car. Opportunities opened up for the average man. Bill was able to use his four weeks' vacation to travel extensively, once an activity reserved for the rich. In retirement, he does a lot of volunteer work because, as one of the "Greatest Generation," he knows how to be of service.

# FAITH TO CARRY THEM THROUGH

*Frederick T. Seifert,*

*As told to Karan Kranz*

Throughout the military history of the United States, the country has
been defended by the young. This was especially true for the United
States during World War II, when millions of boys either enlisted or were
drafted as young as age eighteen. As a result, a generation of Americans
was quickly thrust into adulthood. To get them through this tumultuous
transition, further complicated by the brutality and horrors of war, many
of these young soldiers, remarkably, turned to faith in God. One such
soldier was Frederick T. Seifert.

Fred was born on February 21, 1925, in the Pittsburgh suburb of Penn
Hills. He attended Corpus Christi grade school, "a good fine Catholic
school," as Fred notes. He continued high school in the Catholic tradition
by attending Central Catholic High School. Despite his good grades, Fred
quit school and enlisted in the United States Navy on February 20, 1942,
one day before his eighteenth birthday. Knowing that he would enlist on
his birthday anyway, his parents reluctantly consented and signed to give
their permission. He was "gung-ho" to fight the "Huns" and the "Japs."
Fred was not the only young man eager to enter the war. "Everybody
seemed to want to get in because you don't know what war is like, you
just wanted to go," Fred says. "In fact, you went down with your buddies,
and if they failed, they were upset. One kid actually cried because they
wouldn't take him," he recalls.

Many thousands of area recruits left Pittsburgh for military training through the Pittsburgh & Lake Erie Railroad Station of 1898. In keeping with the blackout, its stained-glass skylights in the Grand Concourse were painted over. The P&LE building is now part of Station Square. *Carnegie Library of Pittsburgh.*

Fred took a train from the P&LE Station and headed for boot camp. This was only the second time in his young life that Fred had been in downtown Pittsburgh.

His family had no car, and he had been sheltered and rather isolated. It was not until he arrived at Great Lakes Naval Training Center for boot camp that he realized how naïve he truly was. Fred remembers his embarrassment during a thorough physical exam. He says, "The shock of my life I think was that you had to strip. You had to be completely naked. I'll never forget. You had a folder with all your IDs and everything. And where do you think I was holding mine?" Perhaps worst part was not knowing when to be embarrassed. Fred's blushing face, when telling another story,

Pittsburgh-area inductees undergoing a physical exam. These men are seeking admission to the U.S. Army Air Corps, which had higher educational requirements and a top age limit of twenty-seven. The Pittsburgh Examining Center experienced a higher application rate than other cities. *Carnegie Museum of Pittsburgh.*

demonstrates his inexperience when he left for the war. "So they're checking this, they've been checking that, and I had to go and talk to this one guy. I didn't know what a psychiatrist was. So I go in there and he says, 'Are you ashamed of yourself?' I said no. Oh, but first he said, 'Did you ever kiss a boy?' Like an idiot, I said 'yeah,' thinking of my dad or something like that. Then he said, 'How about a girl?' I said, 'Well I'm not too good at that!'" Still shaking his head sixty years later, Fred admits he didn't understand what the doctor was getting at. It didn't occur to him until later.

Anatomy and sexuality were not the only things that were new to young Seifert. He encountered new daily routines and a harshness to life he had never experienced before. Fred describes his first morning in the chow line where, to his amazement, they had baked beans for breakfast. He had never heard of eating such a thing in the morning. "You don't eat baked beans for breakfast," he remembers thinking with astonishment. Later that day, they had bean soup for lunch. Fred also recalls the difficulty he had adjusting to new sleeping arrangements, using hammocks instead of beds. He and some of his peers had trouble balancing in the hammocks. Therefore, the group would sleep on the floor. This adaptation proved a suitable solution until Chief Petty Officer Ripley discovered their practice. "He would not tolerate this. You did as you were instructed and not what you thought best. Chief Ripley, wow was he tough." Fred later realized, "That's part of the process of being inducted into the navy." Of boot camp he says, "It was quite an experience!"

After a seven-day leave, Fred remembers being asked what he would like to do. Being young and enthusiastic, all he could think of was action. "Some of us young guys, we were gung-ho. We wanted to go to battle. We wanted to get in as soon as we could on a big ship and fight the Japanese." Therefore, Fred entered an OGU (outgoing unit) and headed cross-country for two weeks of gunnery training at Treasure Island Armed Guard Center, near San Francisco. Fred describes how once there, "They said, 'You are in the armed guard.' And I said, 'What in the world is the armed guard?' I don't want to guard something. I'm thinking I'm going to be guarding something like a building." Later he realized this meant he would be a gunner on a merchant ship.

Next, Fred headed for anti-aircraft training at Point Montana, California. He recalls training drills where biplanes flew overhead pulling a sleeve, which gunners aimed and shot at. "A couple of the guys were so young and naïve that they were shooting at the biplane! Up in the tower they yelled, 'You dumb blankety-blanks! You don't shoot at the biplane, you shoot at the sleeve!'" Despite such errors, most of the young sailors received ship assignments after training. On June 15, 1943, Fred was sent to Portland, Oregon, and was assigned to the SS *Ephraim W. Baughman*, a new Liberty ship from the Henry Kaiser shipyard. From Portland, Fred went to Long Beach, California, to pick up supplies. The trip was also a "shake-down cruise." "We were assigned to take trucks, jeeps and other equipment to India. Of course we didn't know at this point it [the destination] was India where the cargo would help build the Burma Road." Fred remembers they took so many supplies that every available space on the ship was used for storage. The ship was packed, cargo holds were filled and "stuff was even on the deck."

The *Baughman* ready, Fred and his shipmates sailed to Wellington, New Zealand, where they refueled and obtained water, and then to Perth, Australia, where they got orders. Next the ship sailed to Colombo, Ceylon, where they dropped off supplies to make the ship lighter so they could navigate the Hugli River to their final destination, Calcutta, India. During the journey the sailors were warned that many of the surrounding islands were occupied by the Japanese. They were given strict orders to sound general quarters if they saw anything suspicious. Fred recalls, "So I'm up on the bow and I'm looking out at the water and I saw something in the water on the horizon, and I said, 'My God, what's that?' I said, 'It has to be a plane.' I pushed the alarm for general quarters. Everybody was running to their battle stations and all of a sudden it flapped its wings. It was an albatross! I was never so embarrassed in all my life." Inexperience was no excuse for such a mistake. As a result, Fred adds, "boy I got razzed good!" About a week later in the Indian Ocean, he saw something else but decided against reporting it. Fred explains, "See, I didn't want to make two mistakes. I'd rather die, but I'm not going to make two mistakes in one trip." The bridge did eventually report the object. General quarters were once again sounded. The gunnery officer said it looked like a Jap sub, so they started firing at it. The captain came out, looked and shouted, "It's a sea turtle!" The concerns of the sailors were not unfounded, as they soon saw firsthand. Two weeks before they arrived in Ceylon, the Japanese had bombed the harbor. Ship masts could be seen sticking out of the water.

After leaving Ceylon and going up the Hugli River to Calcutta, Fred found many more life lessons awaiting him. There he encountered an alien Indian culture. He remembers how the people there were either very rich or very poor. "I was surprised by the lack of respect for human life in India." Several events he experienced lent credence to this viewpoint. On one occasion when an Indian shoreman was unloading deck cargo, a large truck fell down and landed on top of the Indian man. As the Americans tried desperately to get the man out, the Indians just sat around. Fred is still shocked by this casual concern for life. He showed a concern for human life in the face of the many who lacked it. One evening a bunch of the guys went to a "house of ill repute," and Fred went along with them. When he got there, he met a girl who couldn't have been much older than fourteen. He was shocked to see the depths to which some would sink in their struggle with poverty. Even now, with deep emotion he relates, "I felt so bad, I just couldn't do it. So I gave her all the money I had, about a hundred rupees, and waited for the other guys outside." When the guys asked him to join them next time, he said no.

But there was another side to India. Fred learned more about the goodness of people there. Although he wasn't much of a drinker, calling himself a "shameful Irishman," from time to time he would go out with the guys. On one particular occasion, he left behind several of his personal possessions at the nightspot. Once he realized he had lost the items, Fred thought for sure that they were gone. The next morning, much to his surprise, there was a poor little Indian boy standing outside the ship with his things. Fred stood there, amazed that this boy who had nothing would return his stuff. His eyes begin to swell with tears as he continues to recall how he took the little boy out to buy him some new clothes and gave him his remaining rupees. The money and clothes he gave seemed to be the least he could do in return for the lessons that he had learned.

From Calcutta, the *Baughman* went back to Ceylon. There, Fred notes with a tone of shame, he went out with a few of his buddies and came back with a tattoo of a navy symbol. Perhaps it was an act of camaraderie, possibly a moment of rash fun or a way to escape the intensity he encountered in India. It was not why he got a tattoo but more what he had tattooed that bothers Fred. As he rolls up his sleeve to reveal the tattoo on his arm, he explains that it was an English navy symbol, not an American one. "So young, I never thought to explain [to the tattoo artist] which navy symbol." This mistake was one he would keep quiet when he returned home, particularly because of his Irish background. "My mother would have killed me," he notes with a stern face.

The fleet left Ceylon and went through the Suez Canal to Alexandria, Egypt. Then they crossed the Mediterranean Sea on their way to the Straits of Gibraltar. Of this leg of his journey Fred recalls, "We were warned that the Germans were disguising themselves as Swedish merchant ships. Of course being young, you're looking at everything." It was not until they pulled into Alexandria, however, that Fred and his fellow sailors saw their first German bomber. Even though the plane was out of range, Fred admits, "everyone wanted to fire. You wanted to get into battle. Here we are, we didn't even know." The sailors remained alert through the Mediterranean as news of a supposed alliance between France and Italy spread. Fred heard rumors that France might send spies out to attach bombs to Allied ships. Thus, his ship dropped depth charges off the sides as they went through the Mediterranean to blow up any possible subs or spies. Once past Gibraltar, they crossed the Atlantic for home.

Despite all the dangers, Fred "made it all around the world, twenty-five thousand miles," entering the port of Baltimore. Although they were back in the United States, Fred recalls that they were quarantined during Thanksgiving. They were given an elaborate spread, but Fred most vividly recalls he "drank milk until it was running down [my] chin." He was quite fed up with powdered milk. Finally, on December 6, 1943, he was released from quarantine.

Following his twenty-day leave in Pittsburgh, he was sent to an armed guard station in Brooklyn, New York. On January 5, 1944, he received his next assignment to the SS *James Lykes*, a C2 ship (an all-purpose cargo ship, noted for speed). Leaving from an ammunition depot in New Jersey, he knew they would be carrying explosives. What Fred says he did not know was how expendable the navy considered them to be. As the convoy crossed the Atlantic, headed for England, he said the *Lykes* always traveled in the corner of the formation. He now believes it was to prevent a hit on the *Lykes* from taking out the rest of the convoy. Fred also remembers the ships using flags and lights for communication to keep the enemy from picking up their radio signals. Once in England, the ship stopped at the east coast town of Hull and London to deliver the bombs. By the time he was in London, Fred says he was due for a second leave. However, an officer told Fred he was to round up six of his best men to go on a troop transport ship for the invasion of Normandy. Again Fred recalls feeling young and expendable, as he learned that they were not necessarily the best or the brightest but they were single. "We ran into the six married men we were replacing when we got on the ship and they were getting off." Nonetheless, Fred Seifert became a third-class petty officer and gun captain assigned to the SS *Lee S. Overman* on April 17, 1944.

The *Overman*, carrying fusiliers or British infantry, headed down the Thames River. Fred thought they were heading for Calais, France, where many thought a battle would occur. To his surprise, however, they sat out in the open in the Thames Estuary for several days. "They [British infantry] were aboard for a couple of weeks. And we thought, 'What in the heck? Why would we have them this long?'" Fred noticed that on the English shore, "what they had were tanks and trucks, but there was one thing…they weren't real!" This inflatable weaponry on shore, he realized, were decoys. In addition, they were given very specific rules of engagement. Fred describes, "We were told [if we saw] any aircraft coming over, German aircraft, 'do not fire at them unless they come at you.' In other words, if they are flying over you, let them see you."

While it did not occur to him until later, like the tanks on southern England, they, too, were serving as decoys. "We were put out there for bait," Fred exclaims, furthering his notion that young sailors were expendable to the navy. Fred admits that the decoy worked. Hitler expected Allied troops at Calais, the closest point from England to France. To the west, in Southampton, the real invasion force was embarking. Fred

Happy New Year, Adolf!          —By Hungerford

The New Year's Day issue of the *Pittsburgh Post-Gazette* featured a cartoon by the city's beloved Cy Hungerford. This cartoon gives strong warning of the D-Day invasion, still more than five months away. *Senator John Heinz History Center.*

recalls how after their stint as decoys they headed to Normandy, to the primarily Canadian landing point, Juno Beach, to drop off the British troops. June 6 was rapidly approaching, and they realized that they would not make it in time for D-Day. While their fleet hurried toward Juno, German shore batteries fired as they passed single file between the Cliffs of Dover and the Calais shore. "We couldn't see them…we couldn't even fire back because those projectiles, they could hurl those twenty miles or more," explains Fred. Although projectiles were all around, the *Overman* did not get hit; only one ship in their fleet did. Finally on June 8, 1944, two days after D-Day, the *Overman* arrived at Juno Beach in Normandy.

Even though he was a gunner, as part of the new transporter, one of Fred's duties was to take soldiers from the ship to land. This gave him his first real glimpse of the tragedy of war. "When I saw that beach, it was a mess!" Fred says. "My God, there was litter all over the place." Although he was not supposed to get off the landing craft, Fred says, as

LSTs (landing ship tanks) were launched sideways into the Ohio River. From there they were floated down the Ohio and Mississippi Rivers to the Gulf of Mexico. *Senator John Heinz History Center.*

a curious young man, he ventured off a few times to see the excitement. "You could see the bursting of shells," Fred remembers. "You could hear everything. The planes going overhead. It was like a real war scene. I don't think you realize you are going through it at the time because you're so keyed up." A burly beach master instructed the men: "Get off the beach. Keep moving inland! You don't stop! There are only two kinds of men here, the living and the dead. If you're living, keep movin'!" The troops did not always heed such directions. Oftentimes, the men would gather souvenirs among the debris. Fred collected a Thompson submachine gun, German projectiles and a German belt. Fred recalls, "I picked up the stuff and thought, 'I'm gonna bring it home.' But what the hell am I gonna do with a Thompson submachine gun? Well, it ended up in the ocean because I got scared. They had this thing that, when [we] were coming back, not to bring anything. So I threw it all! And I could have snuck it in…but I was naïve."

War paraphernalia did not turn out to be the souvenirs he brought home. The reality of dead soldiers and the humanity of the enemy were the "souvenirs" Fred took home and would never be able to get rid of. He has two other memories of Normandy. "To this day I do not like sardines," Seifert states. "I saw a can of sardines [at Juno] and I saw these soldiers. They were just floating, bobbing up and down. I said to my friend George [of one soldier], 'Hey let's pull him out of the water!' And look, he had a little hole here. Well, the sergeant major said, 'Roll him over.' Well, the whole back of his head was missing. But he had a can of sardines and pictures coming out of his knapsack. The pictures I put back in his knapsack as we propped him up on shore. But I thought, 'He won't eat these sardines, I'll take them back with me.' You know what, when I went to bite into those sardines, I threw up." As his eyes fill with tears, he continues, "…And today I don't eat sardines…[because] I thought of that."

Fred relates the story of his first encounter with a German POW. "You know you think it's a superman," Fred says. "When you see them, some of them, hell, they're not much different than we are. You don't realize… The first one I saw, he had a crucifix. And I said, 'Can't be…it can't be!' And it was a crucifix, not just a cross. So you're sort of shaken by it. We are fighting human beings no different than we are." After taking a pause to hold back tears and years of emotion, Fred sums up, "Yea, that was an experience…seeing the crucifix."

After the invasion of Normandy, the *Overman* headed back to London. When on the English Channel, Fred saw his first V-1 buzz bomb, on June 12, 1944. "I remember the first one," Fred says. "We fired at it and, God, we misjudged the speed. We thought it was going slow; it sounded like it was lumbering along, but actually it was going three hundred [miles per hour]. And we were missing it, way astern…[But] we didn't know what they were. No idea what they were. Everybody was dumbfounded to find out they were V-1s, which we found out a couple of days later."

Once in London, the ship picked up more troops to take back to Normandy, "which was dangerous because we were crossing that bad spot [in the English Channel]. I couldn't figure out why they were doing that there. But they couldn't have all their troops coming from one place so they had to divide us up." Fortunately, the *Overman* arrived at Normandy safely for the second time. Allied troops were dropped off, and the ship returned to the United States.

After a thirty-day leave, Fred was assigned to the SS *Henry S. Lane*. On September 4, 1944, Fred left New York in a convoy, taking troops to England and then up the Schelde River to Antwerp, Belgium, while the Battle of the Bulge was being fought. He remembers being told, "If you tie up [at] the dock, have somebody ready to leave…you might have to leave in a hurry." This perplexed the sailors at first. Fred describes, "Even the captain couldn't figure out why we would have to leave in a hurry. Then the signal went out and the radio operator found out that the Germans had broken through." As the Germans headed toward Antwerp in an attempt to divide Allied troops, they sent V-2 rockets into the city. "There was no defense against them," recalls Fred. "They were the real rockets. You could see them and then all of a sudden there was a boom. Those things would come in and, man, they hit!" The V-2 rockets caused mass devastation, which Fred witnessed firsthand. He describes a particularly painful memory. "There was a theatre called the Rex Theatre in Antwerp. One of the V-2 rockets hit the theatre and there were some casualties. And the gunnery officer said to me, 'You wanna take some men up and see if any of our boys got it?' Cause they were sure [that they did]." The attack killed over six hundred Americans.

The war was financed not only through heavier taxation but also through the sale of war bonds to the public through patriotic messages. They were promoted through a series of "drives," eight in all, as the need for funding continued. *William J. Gaughan Collection, University of Pittsburgh.*

As he retells the story, the horror of the memory is apparent in Fred's flushed face and broken speech, but he continues: "It was a carnage there. It was a sight that you probably didn't want to see again. Cause there's bodies just torn apart. And now, well you did realize that war was hell, but now you're getting it more and more that it is." While he still knew the enemy was the enemy, the once inexperienced sailor was no longer excited and gung-ho. The reality of war had set in. Fred was more than ready to return to the United States when his duty on ship was completed on June 1, 1945.

Fred then attended ammunition handling school at Camp Peary, Virginia, from October to November 28, 1945. He was sent to a naval ammunition depot in Red Bank, New Jersey. With the war over in Europe, Fred defused bombs in the United States. Here he served until his enlistment ran out on February 20, 1946, his twenty-first birthday. He was honorably discharged with the rank of coxswain.

For Fred, life seemed to grow more difficult once he returned to "normal life." He describes how he lacked a desire to do much and was prone to episodes of anxiety and vomiting. Despite this, Fred finished high school at Taylor Allderdice and then went to Duquesne University on the GI Bill. Still, he had difficulty adjusting to life at home and continued getting panic attacks. Even though he made appointments, he never really wanted to go to a doctor and thus never kept them. Eventually the 52-20 club (twenty dollars a week for fifty-two weeks' readjustment pay) helped him refocus. He also feels that "Duquesne took very good care of veterans." It was there, in a psychology course, he finally realized what was "wrong" with him when he read about post-traumatic stress disorder.

With time, Fred was able to heal his war "wounds." He devoted his life to the education, growth and development of children. He eventually got married and had nine children, raising them in the Pittsburgh area. He also obtained both a bachelor's and master's degree in education from Duquesne University and worked as a teacher and principal in the Penn Hills School District. Since retiring, Fred has spent much time as a volunteer at local hospitals and nursing homes. Fred says that one of the greatest rewards of his service in World War II was that, combined with his Catholic upbringing, he formed a strong moral code. His war experience gave him an understanding of humanity that Fred has continued to employ throughout his life.

# Part III

# Husband and Wife Stories

# OCEANS APART

*James Arthur Krebs and Helen McGrogan Krebs,*

*As told to Helen E. Krebs*

M any soldiers went off to war engaged to loved ones who promised to wait for them, but not too many such engagement stories involved both parties deploying to different theaters of the war. James Arthur Krebs, known as "Art" in the family, served with the U.S. Army Engineering Corps as an officer directing the building of landing strips in the South Pacific, while his fiancée, Helen McGrogan, was a surgical nurse on hospital ships, making sixteen crossings of the Atlantic. They corresponded for three and a half years of wartime service before they were both married in uniform after Germany's surrender.

Art Krebs was the oldest child of German-speaking immigrants who settled in the Southside of Pittsburgh near the turn of the century. Art spoke nothing but German until the time he entered the first grade. His father was an accomplished tailor who set up his own shop in the newly developing neighborhood of Beechview, not realizing that it was never to attract the clientele for custom-made clothing. Still, he was able to establish a reputation that drew customers from all over the Pittsburgh area. Although the family had Americanized, they saw their trade slowed during World War I and purchased a huge American flag to hang from the building, lest customers be suspicious of their German origins. Disaster struck the family when Art's father and his six-year-old sister died in the influenza epidemic at the war's end. Art, age fourteen, grew up fast, as he took on the responsibility for his mother, sister and two younger brothers. Although his education was interrupted by the necessity of full-time work, he graduated in 1931 at the beginning of the Depression from Carnegie Institute of Technology with a degree in civil engineering. Art was the only one of his class to have a job awaiting him, and that was as a clerk in a hardware store. When World War II started, he had his recently lapsed ROTC commission reactivated so that he could serve in the army engineering corps. Art always suspected that FDR deliberately helped facilitate the attack on Pearl Harbor to involve the United States in the war.

Helen McGrogan was the oldest of five children. Her father was a foreman in the mines in West Newton, twenty-one miles southeast of Pittsburgh. Despite her father's death from black lung disease when she was fourteen, the family managed to find the resources to enroll her in a nursing program at Pittsburgh Hospital after her graduation from high

The desperate need for nurses led to accelerated training programs. The cadet nurses of the May 1944 graduation class at Homestead Hospital have already received their uniforms. *William J. Gaughan Collection, University of Pittsburgh.*

school at seventeen. She was working as a nurse at Magee Women's Hospital in Oakland when she met Art while tending to his mother before her death from cancer. Frustrated with staffing shortages, she resigned and enlisted in the U.S. Army Nursing Corps in June 1941. This classified her as "regular army," in service prior to the United States' entry into the war. She was writing Christmas cards when she learned of the bombing of Pearl Harbor.

The Krebs family had kept in touch with Miss McGrogan after their mother's death, so when Art was sent to Indiantown Gap, he knew that Helen was already stationed there. He renewed their acquaintance, and a romance blossomed. Helen invited Art to take her to a dance at the officers' club, and he at first refused and then hurried home on leave to get some dancing lessons from his sister before taking Helen up on the invitation. She had her picture taken in uniform while she was there. Art saw it on display in the photographer's window, promptly bought it and carried it with him all through the war. When her deployment seemed imminent, he stripped his bank account to buy her an engagement ring, knowing that no jeweler would consider giving credit to a soldier off to war. When she accepted, he tried to convince her to marry him, but she, seeing the risks ahead for both of them, asked him to wait until they met again in the same port. He saw her off on the train and thought again about all the young men she would be meeting in the future. Art was granted a leave to take the train to Fort Dix hoping to convince Helen to marry him at once. He found that she had already been deployed to the Port of New York. He arrived there, only to see her ship disembark. In trying to trace her movements, Art attracted the attention of army intelligence, which wanted to know why he was asking so many questions.

Helen served on three different hospital ships stationed in the North Atlantic in the next three and a half years, the longest of these services on the USAHS *Chateau Thierry*, refitted from World War I. As a surgical nurse, she participated in the North African campaign, the Italian invasion and the invasion of southern France.

Although there were times when they operated for thirty-six hours straight following a battle, there were also opportunities to see parts of the world she had only heard about. She enjoyed her leave in England and even made her way to Edinburgh, Scotland, but missed out on seeing

London because of the bombings. She couldn't wait to get ashore and explore Naples and was exasperated with her fellow nurses who stayed on the ship, playing cards in their stateroom. She pulled back the curtains on them, demanding that they look out on the famous Bay of Naples, reminding them that they would probably never be there again. They reluctantly looked and returned to their cards. The eruption of Mount Vesuvius at this time was a great concern to the Allies, who feared that the glow in the sky would make their invasion ships visible to the enemy. Instead, Vesuvius served as a beacon to the Allies navigating the waters to the beachhead.

Helen scoured the bazaars of Morocco looking for items to send back to her family at home. She developed a never-fail system for doing what she wanted on shore. She and a nurse friend would ask their commander to assign them a corpsman to accompany them on leave. The officer would object, "Surely two attractive women like you will have no difficulty finding soldiers to escort you," to which she would reply, "Yes, but then we would have to do what they want, and we want to shop." As Helen browsed the shops, the men assigned to escort duty often purchased duplicates of her selections for their own wives, mothers and sisters. She received grateful letters from relatives who noticed the change in quality of the souvenirs from the "junk" their men usually sent home.

The shipboard community was like a village. Many of the hospital ships even had their own newspapers. There was a proliferation of different "clubs" of like-minded individuals with similar hobbies. There was always a group interested in theater who formed a chorus or performed skits. One night, several days sailing out of New York, the crew was invited to a choral presentation of a new musical entitled *Oklahoma!* The audience was thrilled and uplifted by the story and music. Officers, who had not planned to attend, were drawn in by the music and stood in awe. They were informed that Rodgers and Hammerstein were opening this show on Broadway that very night, and they had seen to it that the ship had received an advance copy so they could enjoy the show along with the New York audience. That musical remained Helen's favorite.

Art had assumed that he would be assigned to the European Theater as well. When he received his commission, as an officer he was responsible for his own uniforms, unlike the GIs who had government-issued uniforms.

All the major stores had military uniform departments during the war. Art purchased his dress uniforms from Kaufmann's Department Store in Pittsburgh, and his wool shirts and heavy, long, wool coat survived the war in pristine condition. He ended up with an assignment in the Pacific Theater. Art served with the 198th Engineer Aviation Company and the 362nd Engineers, building airfields for army air corps bombers and fighters in islands throughout the South Pacific, including New Caledonia and Tinian.

Art shuddered at the thought of thousand-year-old coral beds that they dug up, deposited on land and crushed to make the landing strips. The lumber shipped across from the mainland was expensive, long-lasting redwood destined for temporary wartime use. He saw shiploads of jeeps and other equipment dumped into the ocean at the end of the war because it was too expensive to transport them back once they had been deemed unnecessary. He reflected that war is all about waste.

World War II exacted an enormous toll on America's resources, including its iron ore deposits. The worker at Jones and Laughlin Steel Corporation's Elizabeth furnace in 1942 is cutting steel beams. *Senator John Heinz History Center.*

War has long periods of inactivity punctuated by bursts of exhausting effort. During the long periods on the hospital ship, Helen learned to knit and crochet, a very difficult accomplishment for her because, as a lefty, she could never learn how from her mother. Handcrafts and needlework were extremely popular onboard ship. The surgeons could not afford to let their fingers get stiff and were constantly working on projects so they would be ready when the time came for surgery. One of the doctors returned home with a complete set of needlepoint chair covers for his wife. Anyone stationed on a hospital ship was sure to leave with extensive dental work and all the elective surgery they needed. The doctors and staff had to stay on top of their game. But when casualties arrived, there was little rest. In that time when they were desperately needed, Helen was grateful for the newly developed sulfa drugs that saved so many from dying of infection. By war's end, they also had the miracle of penicillin.

There were moments of strife as personalities clashed. Helen knew an "egotistical, atheistic doctor who relished in teasing the nurses and reducing them to tears." She had a tendency to snap back with a sarcastic remark and then to run to her superior to tell her side of the story first rather than be accused of insubordination. Her commander always found her justified and extracted apologies from her antagonist. Helen claimed that those professed atheists, who frequently belittled the devout, would be sitting beside the Catholic nurses saying the Rosary when the bombs started falling.

Despite her poor circumstances growing up and her lack of self-confidence in high school, Helen took to command easily. She set up her routines and held her assigned corpsmen to them. Occasionally, someone would interfere with her routine and she would strongly object. One Sunday, she headed out of her unit for Mass and happened to find her corpsmen washing down the walls. She was appalled that they should be working unnecessarily on a Sunday and confronted them about it, only to be told that another officer, seeing them idle, had given them the assignment. Helen immediately hunted up the other officer and, in no uncertain terms, asked why he had interfered with her routine. "Have you ever worked men for twenty-four hours straight, given them coffee and thrown them back in for another twelve hours? Well, I have. These are trained medical corpsmen, not laborers. We have our routine and walls are washed each week according to schedule. Don't you dare interfere with my command again!" When she asked her men why they had started the job in the front room instead of in the back as per routine, they confessed that they were afraid that she might not have seen them until the job was done. If she had to pass them on her way, they knew that she would come to their rescue.

In the Pacific, Art was given African American troops to direct in the work of constructing air bases. Although a few African American units performed heroic service on the battlefield, most were relegated to jobs of manual labor. There had been some previous incidents resulting in bodily harm to white officers, but Art was unaware of this when he assumed his command. He showed up at the mess hall on the first morning and choked on the coffee. One of the other officers asked him, "Is something wrong?" to which he replied, "There certainly is! This coffee is undrinkable." The officer explained that the men were from the South and were used to sweetening the coffee with molasses. They had been asked not to do it, but to no avail. He asked Art if he would like to take on the duties of mess officer along with his assignment. Art agreed and had the molasses out of the coffee by the end of the week. He was very proud of his men. Although sometimes fights broke out among them, he seldom had to interfere. He felt that if you explained the work clearly to them and gave the orders in a dignified way, they always rose to the occasion. They worked hard and were willing to put in long days when the situation demanded. When Art left this assignment, the men personally thanked him for treating them with respect.

Art and Helen both enjoyed good rapport with the officers and enlisted personnel. Neither one of them smoked, so they could afford to be generous with cigarettes that came their way. They each received an officer's liquor ration, but since they both drank in moderation, they always had extra bottles to give or trade for favors. They felt that many of the officers drank too much, especially out of loneliness, sometimes leading to fatal mistakes. The only time Art got drunk was at a party he hosted to celebrate his promotion to captain.

In her wartime journal, Helen often recorded that she felt lonely and missed home. She also missed Art and wondered where he was and what their future would be like together. When they had a chance or were particularly lonely, they wrote to each other. In the first six months of the war, Art wrote Helen over fifty times. The contents of their letters were very strange. They could not write anything that would divulge their location, assignment or future deployments. They also didn't want to worry the other about safety concerns. So Helen's letters referred to entertainments on shipboard and Art's told of little projects like scrounging up scraps of wood to build a tent floor and a circular table around the center post. They both wrote extensively about their plans for a future together, picturing the family they intended to have and even suggesting names for children not yet conceived. Times of crisis and danger were entirely left out. If Art found it hard writing letters that wouldn't be marked up by the censors, it was even worse when he had the censorship duty for the men on one of the islands. He was embarrassed to be reading their personal correspondence and having to obliterate passages. There is little privacy in war.

Carrying out a correspondence between two active officers in the military was like shooting randomly and hoping to hit the target by accident. Both were being deployed to different assignments in their specific theaters, so the mail had a hard time catching up. On one day, Helen received twenty-two letters from Art, forwarded from previous posts. But there were many times when these cherished letters were all they had to carry them through.

Many of Helen's fellow nurses were single and on the prowl. They were often disappointed to be meeting married men while the single men were clustered around Helen. "Nothing so attracts young men than knowing that you are already taken and they are off the hook." She does remember one young man who was really smitten with her and tried to talk her out of her engagement to Art. He even asked to see her boyfriend's picture. When Helen produced it, he turned away dejectedly. She explains, "He knew that as a young man with no great prospects he could never compete with this older, mature, confident officer." She, herself, rose to the rank of first lieutenant.

Art and Helen were matched in their ability to see things practically and do what was necessary when conditions demanded. During the hard times of the Depression, both families had taken on whatever jobs had to be done because they could not afford to pay for repairs. They brought that same self-reliant, can-do attitude to their military lives. Art proved to be an adept problem solver. He was told at one of his postings that the outdoor shower was terribly cold. They were wondering if he could come up with some kind of heating unit for the large water storage tank. He looked the situation over carefully and told them to place corrugated metal sheeting over the water tank so that the heat of the tropical sun would warm the water. It worked perfectly.

Art was very observant as well. As he was walking one evening, he noticed a house on a hill with a flickering light. He originally thought that the light bulb was not screwed in completely so that it was only making intermittent contact, but when it was still flickering the next evening, he reported it to the command with his appraisal of the situation. Sure enough, the owner of the house was a Japanese sympathizer who was sending coded signals to a submarine offshore. The man was quickly apprehended.

Helen was noted for her surgical set-ups, where everything necessary for the procedure would be available on the tray for the surgeon. In one particular case, however, the doctor needed an unexpected instrument. Helen informed a nearby corpsman of what was needed and instructed him to get it from the autoclave, the sterilization unit. He came back shortly afterward to tell her that the autoclave had not cooled enough to be opened and he was unable to obtain the necessary piece. She informed him that "this cannot wait," hurried out of the operating room, took hold of the handle, yanked it open and returned with the instrument. The corpsman was stunned that this relatively small woman had forced the autoclave open when he, a fairly sizable man, was unable to budge it, but he attributed the feat to her high level of adrenaline.

Art had his share of dangers and hardships. He and his men suffered through tropical storms so strong that they sent the corrugated metal roofs of the hangars and storage buildings flying, encountered occasional Japanese snipers holed up on the islands and struggled with construction problems, material shortages, mosquitoes, swollen rivers and a host of diseases. Everyone slept under netting and took the government-issued quinine regularly to fight malaria. Although logistics did an incredible job supplying troops all over the world, there were occasional supply shortages. After a particularly long stint with no fresh fruits or vegetables,

Art, who could never tolerate raw onion, remembered eating an onion like an apple when supplies finally arrived and enjoying every bite.

Hospital ships and camps were responsible for the care of injured prisoners of war. They were kept in separate, guarded wards but given the same treatment, the same access to medical supplies and the same food as the American soldiers. While stationed on shore at a camp in North Africa, Helen discovered that her Italian prisoners who were bedfast were not receiving their meals. She saw to it that everyone who could not make it to the mess hall would be served by the corpsmen. Later, when she was overseeing German troops, she went around with an interpreter, asking the men, "Have you eaten?" They all shook their heads in the affirmative. One of the wounded officers came to her to ask about the questioning. When she said that previous bedfast patients had not been fed, the officer responded, "They were Italian. We are Rommel's men. We take care of our own. None of us who can walk will eat a bite until our fellow soldiers in bed are fed." She had great respect for the Germans and their esprit de corps. General Rommel, the Desert Fox, was known not only for his daring strategies but also for his elite fighting troops.

Each ward was responsible for preparing its own food. When a shipment of prime beef arrived, Helen gave instructions for steaks to be fried up for all the patients, including the POWs. As the beautiful steaks were placed in front of the German prisoners, they became suspicious, thinking this had to be a last meal before execution. Helen explained, "We have received a huge shipment of meat. We are in a desert land with limited refrigeration. We have two choices: serve it now or throw it away. You certainly don't think we should waste it, do you?" Since they had lived on canned rations prior to capture, they happily accepted the steaks.

Each of the Allied nations had to house its own prisoners of war. This raised much difficulty as the war started to turn against the Axis powers. The enemy wanted to make sure that they surrendered to the Americans, when hope of victory was lost. The Americans explained to them that they would be shipped to the United States and possibly farmed out as laborers to ranches and farms in Texas and the Midwest if they volunteered. That suited the young captives very well as they had heard about the Wild West and the cowboy way of life. Many greatly

On the homefront, meat was among the scarcest of rationed commodities. This March 28, 1943 issue of the *Pittsburgh Sun-Telegraph* identifies the shopper as "one of the lucky ones." *Carnegie Library of Pittsburgh.*

enjoyed their time in the United States, grew very close to the families for which they worked and often were hosted by those families when they applied for American citizenship after the war. Those who were captured by the Russians fared badly. Helen says that there was some scandal about Americans backing off at the end of a campaign and allowing the Russians to take prisoners.

As the war drew to a close, Helen and Art were anxious to be reunited. Germany surrendered, and Helen was sent home to await the refitting of her ship for the Pacific Theater. Art, who was due leave, learned that she would be home and pulled every favor he could to puddle jump his way across the Pacific, sometimes sitting for hours on a cargo box because there were no available seats on the planes. They were reunited in Pittsburgh and married within two weeks, on June 16, 1945. Helen had a summer uniform, but Art found the day very hot in his wool uniform bought for the European campaign and barely worn. Her mother gathered roses from her gardens to take to the florist since there were no flower shipments for

First Lieutenant Helen McGrogan and Captain James A. Krebs were married in uniform on June 16, 1945, only a month after Germany's surrender. *Helen McGrogan Krebs.*

the entire war. They had an extended leave together, during which time Japan surrendered. Helen learned that the war was over, that she was pregnant and that a relative had died in a traffic accident all on the same day. With her pregnancy confirmed, she was discharged in October 1945 and was finally able to join Art in Florida. He was placed on terminal leave in October and couldn't wait to take his bride back to Pittsburgh as soon as she was discharged. He was officially discharged in March 1946.

Art made quite a name for himself as a problem solver in civil engineering. He worked for Dravo Corporation and later for Peter F. Loftus Corporation, often on loan to other companies that needed help with structural problems. Helen kept her nursing credentials valid but settled into raising five children and using her expertise to assist family members as a private duty nurse during hospital stays and to help in neighborhood emergencies. Unlike many veterans who suppressed their war memories, as noncombatants, Helen and Art had more good memories than bad ones and spoke of the war frequently. They carefully packed away their army paraphernalia, and they decorated their house with souvenirs they had collected from all over the world. They both kept contact with several war friends. One of Helen's friends, Edna Buzzard McElheny, known as Buzzy, moved into the same developing neighborhood in Upper St. Clair, continuing a friendship that lasted the rest of her life. Another good friend, Margaret Jane Moore, married Art's brother and became a sister-in-law. Because she had cared for so many pilots during the war, Helen did not take her first plane flight until 1970, claiming that she knew these pilots when they were young daredevils and that "those who survived the war are now flying commercial planes." They engaged in many activities with their children, but both had spent too much time in tents during the war to find family camping enticing. Art and Helen wore army fatigues for heavy jobs in the building and maintenance of their house and yard. Their youngest son, when first hearing the expression "Your mother wears combat boots!" when he was in grade school, responded, "How did you know? She only wears them in the garden." For both Art and Helen, the war was an enriching and maturing experience that gave them pride in the service they were able to render to their country. It also tempered them for the challenges they faced in their life together.

# World War II in Pittsburgh, City and County

*Ed and Rose Campbell,*

*As told to Justin Hoffman*

Edward Campbell grew up in Oakdale, a coal mining community ten miles west of downtown Pittsburgh. It was primarily rural, and there were none of the developments that would come into existence in the postwar years. He and his future wife, Rose, shared many similar experiences in World War II America. They vividly remember their reactions to hearing the news of what happened on Sunday, December 7, 1941. Ed recalls how his family had just gotten back from church. They heard on the radio that the American base in Hawaii had been attacked by the Japanese. More details of the attack emerged as the family gathered around the radio later that night. At the time, he was thirteen years old and in the eighth grade. In school the following day, his teacher turned on the radio so the class could listen to President Roosevelt ask Congress for a declaration of war on Japan and describe the "Day of Infamy." In the coming days following the declaration, Ed began to see the movement of troops toward Pittsburgh. His school was at the intersection of Routes 22 and 30, and he witnessed the mass convoys of troops on the way east. "Back then, Route 30 was the main passage through Pittsburgh if you were coming from the west and heading east." He remembers that these troops were coming from posts in the Midwest to guard the East Coast

The day after Pearl Harbor, applicants jammed the navy recruiting office. The *Pittsburgh Post-Gazette* said that in Pittsburgh, applications to the navy exceeded those to the army or marines. *Carnegie Library of Pittsburgh.*

from attacks by the Germans. All roads were closed to civilian traffic as the convoys passed. The teacher had no hope of getting the children away from the window to teach class. He remembers it vividly because it "was quite an experience for a kid who was thirteen years old."

Ed remembers young men lining up at recruiting stations all over Pittsburgh. "All of the eighteen-year-old boys the next day went to the Carnegie recruiting station to join." Ed says the town of Carnegie had the closest recruiting station. "Some kids 'forged' their [parent's] name, like Audie Murphy did, so they could join when they were sixteen. You had to have your parent's signature to join when you were seventeen. There were a lot of parents who had no problem doing that. However, if you didn't join up, most just waited to turn eighteen to be drafted. Everybody backed the government and came together, and no one questioned anything." He pointed out that he had a friend, Conrad Zizinski, who

Although H.J. Heinz Company continued to produce traditional food product lines, it entered new fields during the war. Its Pittsburgh North Side Works also made glider wings with a span in excess of one hundred feet. *Senator John Heinz History Center.*

joined the paratroopers and jumped into Normandy. That friend made a couple more jumps and then joined a glider regiment that later flew wooden gliders into combat. "That guy was my hero," he says proudly.

The male civilian population was greatly decreased by the draft. They were taking a lot of people. Even Ed's eighth-grade math teacher, Howard Robinson was drafted into the navy. He decided to stay in the military after the war. Ed remembers that there were no male teachers left in the school. It was just women who ran the school and taught. His father was also eligible for the draft at the time of the war. "My father was a coal miner," Ed says. "He was thirty-five and a half years old and he received one six-month deferment, which took him past the draft limit of thirty-six." He notes that his father had four children and his occupation was needed because coal was so vital during the war.

Ed talks about going to the movies and watching the newsreels before the film. He liked western movies, "but everybody looked forward to the newsreels about the war." According to Ed Campbell, the audience actually cheered during the newsreel footage. "People were always hanging around until the next show to watch the action again. Everybody was always trying to spot somebody they knew in the newsreels," he recalls. "Sometimes a local boy would actually be spotted in the film and you would see it the next day in the paper."

One unifying phenomenon was the selfless service given by virtually all who lived through this time. Everything from rationing food to collecting scrap metal was expected of everybody. Every man, woman and child knew they had an obligation and asked no questions in helping out a cause they knew to be greater than themselves. "Defense work started up right away and everybody saved everything that they could," Ed remembers. "Everybody took scraps to school and carried it on the school bus, and a truck would come and pick it up. Everybody had to take what they had to school. It wasn't an option to go empty-handed. They took anything, metal, paper, rubber, anything that could be reused."

Young people showed their commitment by buying war bonds. Purchasing these war bonds was a popular thing to do for people at that time, especially children, who would buy stamps that were worth a dime or a quarter and save them. "When you saved $18.75, your war bond would be worth $25.00 after the war," Ed says. Every week they would

Collecting scrap was the principal way in which children could aid the war effort. The students of Lee Public School in Pittsburgh pose triumphantly with 155 tons, the city's largest effort as of October 1942. *Carnegie Library of Pittsburgh.*

Mr. and Mr. James Randolph of Glassport pose in 1944 with thirteen of their fourteen children and their war bonds. One son, not pictured, was serving in the army in Europe. *Carnegie Library of Pittsburgh.*

sell war bonds at his school, and every child had money in hand because it was not an option not to buy the war bonds. "Back in those days nobody had savings accounts, everybody just bought war bonds," he recounts.

Another thing that Ed remembers were the blackout drills that were practiced routinely. His brother, Stewart Campbell, was the air raid warden for Pinkerton Road, close to where his farm was located. They knew when the blackout drills were to take place. There was a building with a siren on it that would alert everybody to cover their windows and turn off the lights when a night drill occurred. "My brother would go up and down Pinkerton Road and make sure everybody had lights out and no one was traveling. To my understanding, Stewart volunteered for the job." Ed's mother volunteered to be a paramedic. Mr. Kramer, a man who ran a business in Oakdale, was teaching first aid classes that Ed's mother attended regularly. Ed even remembers practicing air raid drills in school. When a drill would take place, everyone would go into the hallways or the basement to take cover. Everybody did his part, including the teachers. "If there would have been an emergency during the day, teachers were trained to drive the buses home," he says. "All of those drills went on throughout high school."

Ed dropped out of high school at the age of seventeen. He remembers the exact day: February 24, 1945. Ed went to work in a mill in Carnegie that was doing defense work, like every other mill in the area. All the mills had been switched over to wartime production. The first job he had was to make lids for bomb boxes. Bombs would be placed in these boxes and covered with the lids they were making. They were then transported overseas in military aircraft. When his mill had made enough lids, they began to make end connectors for tanks. The tanks in the South Pacific were having trouble going through swamps and harsh terrain. These end connectors would be attached to give the tanks more leverage going over tough obstacles. They also made porcelain signs to replace metal ones at his mill. These signs are all but extinct today but were used very often back then.

Ed says there were no labor issues in the mill during the war. It was difficult to staff the mills that took up defense work due to the worker shortage. "The mills were going twenty-four hours a day and couldn't even get enough people to work them because so many of the young people were going into the service. Many immigrants were hired, and they fit right in with everybody else. There were no issues regarding the immigrants at home or at work." Carnegie became a very ethnically diverse area because of its industrial character. Ed says that management was deeply concerned about safety. "There were lines painted on the floor so everybody knew that no matter what, you were not to step past that line or you could get seriously injured," he recounts. He just laughs at mention of the iconic Rosie the Riveter. He thinks it funny because his wife's name is Rose and she was always called that. Ed says, "Every woman who worked in the mill was called 'Rosie.' They worked alongside everybody else with no problems. In fact, many stayed on and worked in the mills after the war. Most of them got married to millworkers at some point, but there were some that stayed on and worked."

Many remember the stars hanging in the windows of those families who had loved ones in the service. A blue star meant that the family had a son or daughter in the service, and a gold star meant that they

A female carpenter, one of many "Rosie the Riveters" serving Pittsburgh's war industries, operates a drill press at Robertshaw Thermostat Company. *Carnegie Public Library.*

had died in the service. He notes that these stars were everywhere, and he has sympathy for the poor mothers who had to deal with the loss of their sons. "Everyone had stars hanging in their windows, and some even had three or four stars in the window. Quite a few did that," Ed says. "Everyone was patriotic and backed the government 100 percent. The only ones who questioned the war were the mothers who lost young sons over there."

Rationing was a very important part of the war effort on the homefront. Ed remembers that everyone felt the ration books were a "fair way of doing it." He admits that people knew how to get extra things on the black market, but most stuck to the government-controlled rationing system. Gasoline was the main thing that people needed. Everyone knew of the "certain" local gas station where one could go and purchase extra gas without a stamp. Ed's brother Stewart had an H sticker for his tractor.

471|424 AM

UNITED STATES OF AMERICA
OFFICE OF PRICE ADMINISTRATION

**WAR RATION BOOK FOUR**

Issued to ___*Edward M. Campbell Jr.*___
(Print first, middle, and last names)

Complete address ___*Box 174*___
___*Oakdale Pa.*___

**READ BEFORE SIGNING**

In accepting this book, I recognize that it remains the property of the United States Government. I will use it only in the manner and for the purposes authorized by the Office of Price Administration.

*Void if Altered*      *Edward M Campbell Jr.*
(Signature)

*It is a criminal offense to violate rationing regulations.*

OPA Form R-145                                          16—35570-1

Ed Campbell's war ration book. Note the book required the signature of the person to whom it was issued. *Edward Campbell.*

This sticker allotted him plenty of gas because farmers used a lot more gas than the average person. Farmers were deemed to be very important to the war effort and always had enough gas. "Universal Oil Company would come fill up my brother's gas pumps. Because he had two of his own next to the barn, he had more than enough gas to get by during those times. I remember there was a story in the paper about a station in Pittsburgh that turned in a bunch of H stickers that only farmers used. How many tractors could drive on the North Side of Pittsburgh? Despite stuff like that, everybody thought it was fair. The OPA [Office of Price Administration] set the price on it and everybody got the same amount. They also set prices on things like butter and cheese, but gas was the big one that everybody wanted. Everyone also wanted dairy products and meat. If you had a lot of one thing and none of another, you would just trade with your neighbor."

In the spring of 1944, Ed recalls how people felt that something big was about to happen. All of the troops in England seemed to be mobilizing and getting ready for the invasion of France. And on June 6, 1944, it happened: D-Day. He notes that the significance of the moment was felt around Pittsburgh and that everybody stayed inside and listened to the reports on the radio. "We lost a lot of friends that day. I knew a paratrooper that died, shot while he was still in the air, jumping into Normandy. It was a sad day," he says. Despite losing so many friends, he never saw that official U.S. military vehicle pull up to anyone's house to deliver the dreaded news.

In the summer of 1944, Ed went to work on his brother's dairy farm. He recalls hearing reports of the war on the radio. Specifically, he remembers one reporter named Edward R. Murrow. He says that Murrow reported from Britain when they were being bombed. Everybody knew who Murrow was and listened to his reports every night on the radio. He was viewed as a very courageous reporter because he did not take cover but chose to cover the story from the front lines.

As for President Roosevelt, Ed puts it simply: "They didn't want anybody else in there." The people trusted him and loved everything about the man. Many people knew he was ill, but they thought he would live to see the end of the war. Ed thinks his social programs were popular. "Nobody had a problem with him running for four terms."

During World War II, Dwight D. Eisenhower, Matthew Ridgway, Omar Bradley and George S. Patton became household names. This was a source of pride for the American people, and they were looked upon as great men who did great things for their country. The war ended with the introduction of the atomic bomb. "Some people were against the way Truman ended the war," Ed relates, "but the way I see it, we didn't have a choice. Who knows how many lives we would have lost if we invaded Japan? Many people were still very angry about Pearl Harbor, and their feelings were 'Get rid of them Japs.'"

Toward the end of the war, Ed turned eighteen and received his draft notice. However, the next month Congress ended the draft, so Ed missed going into the service. When the Korean War started up just a few years later, the draft picked up where it left off during World War II. He was one of the first drafted for the Korean War.

Ed Campbell's wife, Rose, grew up on the North Side of Pittsburgh. She was about eight years old when the war started but has a remarkable memory of what happened during the war. She has many memories similar to Ed's. However, because she was growing up in the city, there were some very interesting differences.

Unlike Oakdale, blackouts in the city were very strict. They often came without warning. There were many steel mills that were very close by, and they were considered strategic targets for the enemy. The entire city was aware of this, so they were very disciplined during drills. "All the lights in the homes had to be turned off, and you couldn't turn them back on until you heard the siren again. The air raid wardens actually went up and down the streets with their flashlights checking all of the houses."

Her parents were Ukrainian immigrants who instilled a hardworking mentality in their family. Her brother was a machinist when the war first broke out. She said that many people, such as her older brother, received

The light from the streetcar safety island in Grant Street pierces the darkness during the air raid blackout of October 27, 1942. *Carnegie Public Library.*

deferments because they had a skilled trade. "My brother didn't have to go into the service because he was exempt. He received two deferments, and they told him his expertise was needed in the mill. He never sought out those deferments, but he was just given them. It got to a point where he just couldn't take it anymore because all of his buddies had enlisted. So he went and enlisted in the marine air corps."

She remembers how everyone was so patriotic during that time. "Having stars hang in your window was like a banner. We had two gold stars on our street. Everyone knew who they were and how they were killed," she recalls.

The inner city of Pittsburgh was extremely diverse with many immigrants. Rose relates a story that seemed to reflect the mood of some Americans when the war started. "There was no difference in ethnicity regarding work. Everybody went to work no matter where you were from. There were some who resented the Germans. There was an incident with a girl around my age who lived across the street from me. She and her siblings attended school and church at a 'Bohemian' Catholic church called St. Wenceslaus. One day the father went to a service at the church and he was told not to come back because he was German and had a very German name. They were told to attend St. Mary's, which was looked upon as the 'German' Catholic Church." Other than that incident, Rose remembers people of all cultures being friendly to one another. She feels that people were comfortable in their own ethnic communities. She explains that immigrants settled in an area of the city, and whenever their friends and family came over, they settled in the same neighborhood. But according to Rose, neighbor helped neighbor regardless of where they were from or who their family was.

As for rationing in the city, she remembers that dairy and meat products could "get scarce once in a while." Almost everybody followed the prices that the OPA set, so everybody got a fair share. She relates, "During the war is when they started to use margarine. There was a little button of coloring that you squeezed to give the margarine its color. Some people got scared and thought that the coloring made you sick, but that wasn't true."

There were buildings set aside on the North Side where children could take paper and metal to recycle. They called all of the kids who helped out with the effort "commandos." She says, "The more scraps you brought to them, they gave you an emblem. But we would have done it anyway even if we got nothing in return. It was also like that buying war bonds. You had to have that money once a week."

Rose has vivid memories of propaganda during the war. She recalls that one could not turn a corner without seeing posters. Uncle Sam posters and the anti-Japanese and anti-German posters were all over town. These posters had different pictures on them about the sneakiness of the Japanese and the ruthlessness of the swastika-bearing Germans. She remembers the patriotic music of the time. Songs such as "White Cliffs of Dover," "There's a Star-Spangled Banner Waving Somewhere" and "God Bless America" were all very popular and very inspirational during the war. They saw newsreels of Bob Hope entertaining the troops overseas. Local people got involved in USO events in Pittsburgh by organizing dances for the soldiers where they could go and meet young women.

Parades honoring the nation's military attracted large crowds. Such events helped build enthusiasm for the war effort. This parade is on Fifth Avenue in Pittsburgh's Uptown neighborhood. *Carnegie Library of Pittsburgh.*

Although Ed had remembered listening to Edward R. Murrow on the radio, Rose listened to Gabriel Heatter every night. He was a famous newsman, noted for his catchphrase, "There's good news tonight," who had a nightly show that was popular nationwide. "It's not like today when you can find out what is happening right away," Rose says. "We didn't know what was happening to the Jews right away because it took a while for it to get to us. After we got that news, so many people felt bad for the Jewish people for what they were going through."

Because she was from the North Side, she has fond memories of the parade that was thrown for "Commando Kelly." Charles E. Kelly from the North Side was nationally known because he was awarded the Medal of Honor for his bravery in Europe. There was a big parade in Pittsburgh on April 25, which was designated "Commando Kelly Day." Rose recalls how everyone was so proud because they were from "Commando Kelly's" neighborhood. Later, the support facility in Oakdale was renamed after him.

Rose also feels that most of the country loved President Roosevelt. She says her parents were very fond of him. She feels that he embodied everything that this country was about. "Everybody adored and trusted him," Rose says. "It was a solemn, sad day when he died."

# EVERYBODY HAD TO DO SOMETHING

*John and Sally Smith Haberman,*

*As told to Heather Newell*

John Haberman's and Sally Smith's post–high school plans were put on hold the minute they learned of the attack on Pearl Harbor. Sally remembers hearing the announcement on the radio in her bedroom and dropping to her knees in prayer. The next day, in a school assembly concerning the attack, John knew he would enlist in the U.S. Navy upon graduation. Sally was equally motivated. "Send the guys; I'll do it" defined her commitment, and that of many others, as she considered her wartime involvement. The Pearl Harbor bombing rekindled many not-so-distant memories for Sally's older sister, Lillian Eakin. She recalled World War I efforts such as throwing money into American flags carried horizontally in parades and giving copper cookware and any gold or silver for war materiel. Changing plans and doing without weren't altogether unfamiliar to these three McKeesport residents, and they understood well the necessity of both.

John's decision to join the navy was partly fueled by his previous experience in the Sea Scouts, a division of the Boy Scouts. The coast guard asked the boys to patrol the Youghiogheny River for any unusual activity or even submarines. The fact that they needed to be on the lookout for submarines—which would have had to first enter the mouth of the Mississippi at the Gulf of Mexico and then make their way up that river, the Ohio River and finally the Monongahela River before

The South Side Works of Jones and Laughlin Steel Corporation, one of the nation's largest producers. The banks of the Monongahela were lined for miles by the works of numerous companies. *Senator John Heinz History Center.*

they could pose any threat to McKeesport—was very improbable. More likely, the coast guard wanted to build a sense of emergency in the young scouts. During their shifts up and down the Yough, they saw little more than riverbanks lined with mills producing war goods twenty-four hours a day. Instead of producing steel for cars and other domestic use, Pittsburgh steel mills were making war materiel such as bullets, bombs, masts and armored plates. "Whether it was ridiculous or not, you did it," John says as a way of underscoring the public's attitude toward the war effort.

"Loyalty, duty, commitment" fueled John's enlistment after graduation. On July 15, 1942, he left for Newport, Rhode Island, while Sally continued working at U.S. Steel. Lillian, a wife and mother, volunteered to register men ages eighteen to forty. Her husband, Louis, was forty years old at the time and operated a family real estate business in McKeesport. She personally registered him for the draft. For Sally, this was a very somber time as she explains, "There was no one left." The rest were waiting to be called. Though Louis Eakin was never asked to serve in active duty, beyond the age of those being called, he managed his own real estate business and that of another man who did fight in the war. Lillian recalls his long hours and the responsibility of essentially running two businesses at once as McKeesport's population boomed due to the millwork opportunities. Lillian speaks of women who would call her personally to ask for her help in finding a place to live. Not only was the availability of existing housing limited, but the building of new homes was at a standstill. With most of the labor force at war or in the mills, a relative's newly purchased pre-cut "Sears house" lay in the yard all winter for want of assembly.

Lillian and Sally's parents were also involved in the war effort. John describes their "sense of preparedness," which doubtless resulted from World War I and Great Depression experiences. Lillian would drive her mother, Eva Smith, to airplane spotter trainings. Taught to identify aircrafts by their silhouettes, she would spend her half-day shifts in a tower on a hill in Elizabeth Township, which was said to be the highest point in Allegheny County. Upon identification, she would phone in the plane's direction and an estimate of

This North Park airplane-spotting watchtower was one of many ringing Pittsburgh. They were manned largely by American Legion volunteers. *Carnegie Library of Pittsburgh.*

its speed. This would then be matched with the log of registered flights and checked for accuracy. In addition, Mrs. Smith and other women met weekly to knit woolen "watch socks." Lillian remembers the women knitting constantly, even in church, and sending the socks for the boys to wear while on watch.

Mr. George Smith, Sally and Lillian's father, also served on the homefront through his role as an air raid warden. Sally, who was still living at home with her parents, remembers the word "WARDEN" imposingly printed on his hat. As such, he organized meetings with other men to plan disaster responses and practice emergency medical techniques. Cots were stored in their basement in case they might be needed for the wounded or sick in the event of an attack. The heightened state of alert, Sally and Lillian remember, resulted from the importance of the Mon Valley and its production capabilities. Occasional blackouts were ordered to keep the location of such a vital industrial area as cloaked as possible. Among the requirements of Mr. Smith's job as warden were his neighborhood rounds to ensure the blackout decree was being upheld. One evening, Lillian's radio wasn't working, so she watched her neighbors' house to see when the blackout time would begin. She'd draw her dark green shades, she figured, when they drew theirs. She distinctly remembers the heavy banging on her front door as the warden on watch that night yelled at her for not complying with the blackout drill. She felt like he was insinuating that she was not supporting the war. She explained her radio troubles and then pointed out her neighbors' house, still clearly illuminated. After he ignored her rationale, and reprimanded her anyway, she "had a good cry." Lillian was still too naive to realize that some air raid wardens reveled in their newfound sense of power.

The pace of day-to-day life accelerated dramatically with round-the-clock work shifts and the expectation that everyone take on volunteer hours and community service. Additional time and energy were consumed in adjusting to food and gas rationing and clothing shortages. The war effort required everyone to purchase gas, flour, sugar, meat and butter with coupons received in the mail. This rationing occurred in every household they knew. "It didn't matter if you were rich or poor," Lillian recalls. Sally adds, "When the sugar came in, everybody ran to the store with their coupon. You had to get it when it was available."

A good-natured clerk at Donahue's, downtown, waits on anxious but patient customers, each hoping that the limited supply of rationed meat would last until their turn. *Carnegie Library of Pittsburgh.*

To supplement their diet, all three remember the victory gardens and the sense of purpose gardening gave to many of the "older fellows" who could not fight on the front lines. No space was left idle or unproductive. Empty lots, wooded areas and even places of high grass were turned into gardens. Lillian and Sally's father tended two gardens. In their estimation, there were victory gardens everywhere, "fields of them."

Although these day-to-day life changes were to be expected by a generation used to the demands of World War I and the Great Depression, the cultural changes were decidedly more unexpected. Lillian and Sally remember their mother's prewar dress as consisting of corsets, stockings, slips and long dresses. During World War II, such customs were not practical, and their ensembles shifted slowly to ones requiring no stockings, as silk stocking production virtually halted. The women painted their legs with makeup, which stained the insides of slips and the fronts of couch cushions. More and more, women were seen in pants. All in all, as John says, "it was a war effort, and everyone supported it."

Having a victory garden was one of the ways in which older Americans could aid the war effort. Here a West Run Road resident tends his extensive garden, summer 1945. *William J. Gaughan Collection, University of Pittsburgh.*

Certainly, the war and its demands often interfered with lives. John and Sally's perseverance through such difficult times resulted in a relationship that only grew stronger. Living in the same area and growing up alongside each other, Sally knew they would eventually marry. "We marked each other from day one," Sally says. "I've known him since I was six years old. We've played together and gone all through school together." In high school, John attended the newly opened McKeesport Vocational School as Sally continued at McKeesport High School. They naturally grew apart through this separation but also due to John's working so much after school, in the evenings and on weekends. In fact, Sally discovered that John had enlisted in the navy through his brother. She asked for John's address and began writing letters daily, a correspondence that culminated two years later in an unforgettable wedding.

They both wanted to get married, but family members felt that, at only twenty years old, they were too young. Also, their families did not want them to get married while John was in the service. Despite their objections, and eventually with their approval, Sally and John decided that on Saturday, August 12, 1944, they would tie the knot, while John was stationed in Boston waiting for the completion of the USS *Lewis* and preparing for his departure to the Pacific. John's schedule allowed them a small window of opportunity, so, without any family or friends, Sally boarded a train to Boston. She had with her the top layer of the wedding cake that she ate with her family the evening before, a letter from her mother and a wedding outfit picked out by her sisters. Lillian reflects, "What an awful thing that was that nobody went with you!" However, Lillian could not have gone with a young son and a newborn daughter. Besides, she adds with a chuckle, she "probably didn't have the money anyhow." Despite the fact that she was going alone, Sally responds, "I didn't care. I was happy I was going."

At the Boston train station, Sally began looking for John in the crowd. A sailor approached and thrust a picture at her asking, "Is that you?" Sally describes the scene with a laugh: "I didn't know him, and I was expecting Jack to be there." He explained that he was a shipmate of John's who had to come instead while John was on duty. Disappointed, she went to the YWCA, where reservations had been made for her. She met John later that evening. The next day, they began to make the necessary marriage arrangements. They met with the chaplain and then the judge. "I didn't have a diamond ring," Sally explains, which would have been the case for many betrothed couples in the 1930s and '40s. Sally and Lillian's generation had to forego many customary engagement and marriage practices. In Lillian's case, she married secretly in 1933—in a dress that cost $6.95—in order for her to continue working. In Sally's case, John had been in the navy for two years and didn't have the opportunity or the funds to buy a diamond ring on his $21.00 per month salary. The judge asked for proof of her parents' approval. John and Sally told the judge about their lifelong friendship and their conviction to marry, but as Sally recalls, "that didn't faze her very much." Sally offered to show the judge her mother's letter, but she had left it at the YWCA. She thought to mention their wedding cake but realized that she had left that behind as well. The judge remained firm and would not grant them a license. John and Sally worried that their wedding, planned for 11:00 a.m. the following day, would not occur. After leaving the courtroom, they met an employee who offered his help. In Sally's words, he said, "If that had been any other judge in the country, you'd have had your license. I'll tell you what. You go over to the license bureau. I'm going to call them up, and your license will be waiting for you." Happily, it was. Just what shenanigans he pulled to effect the granting of a license, she will never know.

The next morning Sally dressed in the outfit her sisters had prepared for her. Although she was marrying in August, Sally's sisters thoughtfully planned ahead for fall. Lillian insists that they wanted her to be able to "get some wear out of it," but the gold woolen dress and the brown suede accessories turned out to be too autumnal for the oppressively "110 degrees in the shade" heat that marked the day. Sally also met her bridesmaid, Betty, that morning. Betty, Sally laughs, "looked more like the bride" in her white dress printed with summery flowers. John asked Betty to be there as Sally knew nobody in Boston and they were marrying at the chapel in the Boston Navy Yard. "Fortunately he had made a great choice because she and I got along beautifully," Sally remembers fondly. John's reply speaks to the simplicity of his selection: "There was no choice about it. She was the only woman there." Regardless of these circumstances, Sally and Betty became friends and even lived together for six weeks while their husbands were on a "shakedown cruise" on the *Lewis* before departing for the Pacific in November 1944. Once John was deployed, Sally returned to McKeesport and to work.

Like all the other women whose responsibilities expanded to include outside-the-home employment, Sally worked in the years before and after her marriage to John. She remembers that "life was reshaped to fit [our] working hours," and John comments on seeing female welders in the navy yard for the first time as "something unheard of!"

Sally's first position at U.S. Steel in the employment office required her to ID all the workers in the mill. She created plastic-encased badges that featured each worker's photo, name and department. In addition, she

In a role unimaginable before the war, a female worker welds a beam at the U.S. Steel Homestead Works, January 1945. *William J. Gaughan Collection, University of Pittsburgh.*

Both Jones and Laughlin Steel Corporation and U.S. Steel Corporation vastly expanded their Pittsburgh facilities in order to meet military demand. The Homestead Works, shown above, was expanded, somewhat controversially, through the demolition of a nearby neighborhood. *William J. Gaughan Collection, University of Pittsburgh.*

made a plastic pendant of sorts with a tiny photo of her "Jack" that she wore as a necklace. The identification system was new to the company and to the McKeesport area. "We didn't know fear growing up," Sally recalls, but with the attack on Pearl Harbor and the widespread concern it created, security was an issue.

Not all working hours were dedicated to this task. In addition to preparing IDs, she also had charge of selling war bonds. She was one of the only women allowed in the mill, as she went there to sell the bonds. A $25.00 bond cost $18.75. After the war, she and John used theirs to buy their first home. In her time at the U.S. Steel employment office, she remembers vividly her clear view of the passing troop trains from the second-floor office window. "When we'd hear the train coming, the other girl and I would run to the window…and we'd just hang out there [waving]!"

A mild Pittsburgh day in January 1944 enabled these women to sell war bonds from an outdoor booth at the U.S. Steel Homestead Works. *William J. Gaughan Collection, University of Pittsburgh.*

Sally continued working following her marriage to John. She was hired as the personal secretary to the superintendent of the galvanizing plant in Versailles Borough. In 1946, her position was eliminated due to the postwar industry restructuring. The plant's production of booms, spars and masts halted, and the facility was sold. She liked her work, but at twenty-three years old, she was happy to leave and was ready to enjoy her role as a wife and soon-to-be mother.

Family had always been the cornerstone of Lillian and Sally's lives. During the war, their focus extended to include all of America and its military. Sally wrote V-mail letters to John daily and also to five other soldiers. Lillian invited servicemen to her home for family meals in an effort to make them feel at home. Sally attended USO functions at Renziehausen Park and served coffee and donuts to the troops stationed

In this poignant undated photograph, an exhausted army private awaits his train to return to base. *Carnegie Library of Pittsburgh.*

at Bettis Airport. The family discovered that they had relatives in England who were willing to provide respites for McKeesport neighbors stationed there. Sally explains this family outreach as a charitable act done in hopes that somewhere "somebody [was] doing it for mine." Certainly, thoughts of family were also on John's mind as he returned home after sailing to the Pacific. He expected to be one of five million soldiers invading Japan, but the atom bomb changed that. During his nearly three-month journey home, after three years of active duty, John remembers thinking, "My children will never have to go through what I went through." He returned home on November 29, 1945, too late for Thanksgiving but to a family giving thanks nonetheless.

# MOON TOWNSHIP MEMORIES OF WORLD WAR II

*Dave Price and Jean Klixbull Price,*

*As told to Jennifer Welsh*

W orld War II affected the lives of almost all Americans. Even young school-age children experienced the war in their own way. When the attack on Pearl Harbor occurred, Dave Price was nine years old and Jean Klixbull was eight. Although they did not meet until after the war had ended, they grew up within two miles of each other in Moon Township, at that time a rural suburb five miles west of Pittsburgh. They met in the seventh grade and eventually married.

David Price was born to Owen and Roberta Price in 1932, the youngest of six children. He grew up on Stoops Ferry Road. Marion Jean Klixbull, born in 1933, was the second-oldest child of Arthur and Mary Klixbull. They lived on Old Thorn Run Road, within walking distance from the Prices. As Jean states, "We lived on one hill, he lived on the other."

Neither Dave nor Jean remembers very much of the war prior to Pearl Harbor, but Dave distinctly remembers an incident where his Aunt Frances had a premonition of the coming war. Sometime in 1938 or 1939, his Aunt Frances and her daughter were visiting Dave's family. From the backyard they saw the aurora borealis in the evening sky. Upon seeing it, he remembers his Aunt Frances commenting that it was a bad omen and a sign that there was going to be a war. Of course, events leading to the war were already underway in Europe by this time and the association of the aurora borealis with the war was merely coincidental. Still, this incident left an indelible impression on Dave.

Although Dave and Jean do not remember much about the Pearl Harbor attack, they do remember their parents hovering around the radio and that there was a lot of excitement. Dave also remembers subsequent big headlines in the newspaper like "PEARL HARBOR ATTACKED" and "WAR WITH JAPAN." They recall that many people were initially suspicious of President Roosevelt. "I can remember people trying to point the finger. They blamed the president, claiming he knew about it beforehand and that he should have done more to avoid it," Jean recollects. With so many isolationists, there was a great deal of suspicion of the president and of Washington. In retrospect, Dave attributes these suspicions to speculation. Conspiracy theories surround many catastrophic events, he muses.

Like most Americans, Dave's and Jean's parents worked in industries that contributed to the war effort. Dave's father worked as a plate and shear operator for the Baltimore & Ohio Railroad. Dave could not remember if the B&O was involved in any specific war effort, but railroads in general saw a dramatic increase in usage transporting military personnel and other war supplies. Dave remembers his mother staying home at the beginning of the war, but sometime during the war she got a job at Homestead Valve. His sister had moved back home since her husband had been drafted into the service. She watched the children while Dave's other sister was at work. Dave could not remember precisely what his mother's job was, but Homestead Valve made ammunition or, as Dave describes them, "large bullet shells" during the war. The company stored the shells in four large caves at the facility. When he worked at Homestead Valve later as an adult, these caves were filled in. Dave's grandfather also worked at Homestead Valve during the war as a guard at the front gate.

In December 1941, when the United States entered the war, the Klixbull family had four young children ranging in ages from ten years to three months. Jean's mother stayed home with her children during the war. Jean's father, Arthur, worked at the Dravo Corporation on Neville Island, where he was involved in the installation of radar on landing ship tanks (LSTs). LSTs were very large naval vessels used for amphibious operations. LSTs were used throughout the war in a number of invasions and campaigns,

Mrs. Grace Augustus, whose son was killed at Pearl Harbor, inspects a forty-millimeter projectile in a Westinghouse Naval Ordnance Plant. She had previously been a cafeteria manager for thirteen years. *Carnegie Library of Pittsburgh.*

including Normandy and throughout the Pacific Theater. Dravo's Neville Island shipyard produced 150 LSTs during the war years in addition to 20 subchasers and minesweepers, 27 gate vessels, 27 destroyer escorts, 46 lighters and barges and 65 LSMs (landing ship, medium).

Though Dave and Jean attended different elementary schools—Dave went to Carnot Elementary and Jean went to Thorn Run Elementary— both remember various ways schools contributed to the war effort. For example, there were defense stamp drives. Students could purchase defense stamps for a dime. They would collect these until they totaled $18.75, and then they would exchange them for a war bond. After ten years, this war bond would be worth $25.00. Dave remembers they would compete in contests among classrooms "to see who had the biggest effort." He also remembers having scrap iron collections. He recollects, "We would search the neighborhood and get all the scrap iron and steel for making tanks, jeeps, airplanes, whatever."

Brentwood High School girls pose for the *Pittsburgh Sun-Telegraph* photographer, May 15, 1942, at the scrap collection site established by the local Kiwanis Club. *Carnegie Library of Pittsburgh.*

As a Boy Scout, Dave remembers gathering milkweed pods. "I remember putting these milk[weed] pods in bags and turning them in to our scout master. They told us that they [the fibers] were used for filling life jackets for the flyers who flew over the waters." His memories are accurate. The United States had originally used floss from kapok trees in the Dutch East Indies (Indonesia) as life preserver stuffing. When Japan gained control of this area in 1942, the United States was forced to find a substitute, and milkweed pods were the solution. All over the United States, children were encouraged to gather milkweed pods for the war effort.

Dave and Jean had a number of relatives who served in the war. Two of Dave's brothers served in the Pacific. His oldest brother, John, was an ambulance driver in the army. Dave remembers his mother receiving a letter from John relating an experience when he was stationed in the Philippines. He was so tired that he decided to crawl under the ambulance to sleep. Apparently, he slept through a major typhoon that hit the islands. It was a story they laughed about at the time. His other brother, Owen, was in the marines and guarded Japanese prisoners. Fortunately, neither brother was injured during their service. They both returned home safely at the end of the war.

Jean had five uncles in the service, all from her mother's side of the family. Her uncles George, Ross and Jim were in the navy, and her Uncle Ralph was in the marines. Her Uncle Tom, related by marriage, was drafted into the army. Jean remembers that furloughs were much-anticipated events, as they did not occur often. She does not, however, recollect any stories about her uncles' experiences since they did not talk about it much when they returned. She does remember being afraid that her father and Uncle Pete might be drafted. Jean comments that even though they both had young children, they knew of other young fathers who had been drafted. Four of her uncles returned from the war, of which her Uncle Tom was the only one who was injured. His legs were severely burned. Her Uncle Ralph was killed aboard the USS *Franklin* on March 19, 1945.

The loss of her Uncle Ralph was a most traumatic experience for Jean. She remembers when he came home on furlough in the winter and that he volunteered for the mission on which he was killed. Ralph was on the *Franklin*, an aircraft carrier off the coast of Japan, when it was attacked by Japanese planes. According to Jean, her grandmother, mother and aunts received a letter stating that Ralph was officially declared missing in action approximately six weeks after the *Franklin* was bombed, but they did not tell the children right away. Jean says that her grandmother, mother and aunts did not believe it at first because there was nothing to prove that he might have been killed. When the family was informed later that Ralph was assumed dead, Jean remembers "crying and crying." She also recalls that later a fellow marine who served with Ralph visited the family and gave them some of Ralph's personal items. She says this confirmed for the family that Ralph had indeed been killed. The marine's stories of the times he spent with Ralph comforted them. Interestingly, years later, Jean's Uncle Jim, who was serving in the navy at the time, said that he had actually witnessed the attack on the *Franklin* from the ship on which he was stationed nearby. Jim did not know his brother Ralph was aboard the *Franklin*, but he claimed to have remembered watching Japanese planes circling the aircraft carrier. The story goes that many aboard his ship wanted to shoot down the planes, but those in command were afraid to break radio silence and expose their own position.

Soldiers were respected by the civilian population. As a child, Jean remembers counting the stars on service banners and flags in the windows of other people's houses, her grandmother having four. Servicemen could ride public transportation and go to the movies for free. Dave remembers that when servicemen would get on the bus, the driver would put his hand over the fare box. And as Jean comments, servicemen were always in uniform when they were out in public. "If you saw a uniform, you

Streetcars were long popular in Pittsburgh, but with the introduction of gasoline rationing, they were even more so. Here a crowd is standing on a snow-covered streetcar "island" on Grant Street in front of the William Penn Hotel, waiting to board a Shannon line car. *Carnegie Library of Pittsburgh.*

looked up to that. [A serviceman was] very revered, regardless if he was in the war or stateside," Dave recalls.

Dave and Jean also have memories of the hardships that rationing imposed on people. Items they remember being rationed were sugar, butter, gasoline, rubber, silk, coffee, tea, meat, lard and shoes. The gasoline rationing did not have much of an impact on Dave's family, however, because they did not own a car at that time. Jean remembers the use of oleomargarine with much displeasure. Since butter was so limited, many people turned to using oleo. In the 1940s, most states had laws against selling pre-colored oleo, so companies sold the white oleo with some form of coloring that could be added. Describing her experience, Jean says, "They'd put a little package of red stuff in there and you had to squeeze it into this…I don't know what." She says her sister Lois, who was only three or four years old, remembers the task of kneading the package to evenly distribute the coloring.

Certain toys, like bicycles, could not be purchased. Both the metal and rubber used to make bicycles were needed for the war effort. Shoes were so limited and of such poor quality that both Dave and Jean remember having to put cardboard in the bottoms of their shoes because they were so full of holes. Nylon stockings were so scarce that some women resorted to applying what Jean and Dave called "leg painting." To supplement their food supply, both Dave's and Jean's families had what many people referred to as victory gardens, but Dave says they referred to theirs as a "survival garden." Both families had always had gardens, but the food limitations made having a garden seem even more important. Despite all the limitations, Jean also claims, "No one complained." Nearly everyone was in the same situation and believed that their sacrifices would hasten the end of the war.

As children, air raid and blackout drills primarily incited fear. Both Dave and Jean remember being told in no uncertain terms what they were to do during one of these drills. According to Dave, each family received a pamphlet explaining air raid and blackout procedures. This information was also posted in the newspapers, and warnings of when to expect the drills were announced on the radio. Jean explains that air raid drills occurred during the day and that children playing outside were expected to run home as fast as they could upon hearing the whistles. Inside the house, they would have to sit patiently until the local air raid warden, Francis Hissam, went by in his car and checked each house and then sounded the all clear. Francis Hissam was the local constable who was mainly in charge, but Dave notes that there were "civilian" air raid wardens as well. During blackouts, all lights were to be turned off, and again the children waited patiently until the all clear sounded. While these drills felt like an eternity for the children, Jean says they probably only lasted a half hour. Neighbors could probably remember the consequence for not following the drill procedures, but Dave imagines some sort of fine was imposed because "they were very strict about it." Apparently Francis Hissam's reputation preceded him and left quite an impression on the young children. Both remember their parents threatening them at various times, "You'd better be good or I'll get Hissam after you!" The fear that Dave and Jean as children associated with the air raid and blackout drills

Pedestrians on Diamond Street (now Forbes Avenue) near Market Square are hustled into an air raid shelter during a daytime drill, November 29, 1942. *Carnegie Library of Pittsburgh.*

most likely came from their fear of getting in trouble with a "mean" police officer, but they were also afraid that they actually could be attacked.

For entertainment during the war, Dave and Jean mostly played outside with their friends or listened to radio programs. On rare occasions, they went to the movies. Before the film would begin, a five- to ten-minute newsreel was shown about recent events. Dave says these "brought you that much closer to the war. Just like TV today, you felt like you were there." He also remembers that many of the movies he saw were about the war, like *Back to Bataan*. He notes that some even used real war footage, such as the film *To the Shores of Iwo Jima*. Jean says her brother Bob went to the movies more often because he was older. He claims they used to have an intermission during the movie to collect money to buy war bonds. While Dave does not remember this, oddly enough, he remembers movie theaters giving away dishes on certain days to entice people to attend.

The end of the war brought a brief period of excitement and celebration. Dave and Jean only remember seeing pictures in the newspapers of the mushroom-shaped explosions produced by the atomic bombs that led to the end of the war. They do remember the exhilaration that followed. Dave sums up most people's feelings, stating, "Everybody was just thrilled because there would be no more killing, no more wars. Loved ones are all going to be coming home. Of course you could buy anything you wanted then: butter, shoes, tires, gasoline. Your greatest fears are over. You're worrying and fear is done with." People took to the streets in celebration. Dave recalls hopping into his sister Mary's car to ride out to the American Bridge Company in Ambridge where her husband worked. One gas station attendant was so distracted by the hoopla that he overfilled the tank, causing gasoline to spill everywhere. As they passed, Dave yelled to him. "Hey, how about some free gas? You're running it all over the place." Jean also remembers the happiness and excitement but notes it was relatively short-lived. "We all got back to normal," she states.

For a child living during this time, the war brought fear, limitations and cooperative spirit. The war was at the center of daily life. It affected every aspect of it, including children's thoughts and actions. Jean primarily remembers fear. Her fears ranged from the very probable—that her uncles overseas would be injured or killed—to the improbable—that the United States would be attacked—to those only a child would have—that

Kaufmann's clock is draped in paper ribbon as joyous revelers crowd Fifth Avenue. This *Post-Gazette* photograph was taken at 7:02 p.m. on August 14, 1945, V-J Day. *Carnegie Library of Pittsburgh.*

she would be caught by the air raid warden, Francis Hissam.

Dave remembers the fear as well, but he also remembers how the war affected his desires and aspirations. He and two other neighborhood boys formed a small club. Their motto was "A nickel a week and we will buy a jeep." With all of the reverence for soldiers and focus on the war, he says that during this time he had dreams of becoming a pilot. Dave did not become a pilot, nor did the boys buy a jeep, although Dave thinks the boy assigned to be the treasurer did buy a BB gun. The limitations imposed by rationing also affected them, but as Jean notes, as children, they probably had an easier time adjusting to the entire situation. They were born during the Great Depression, so scarcity was not a new concept. Jean feels that the biggest impact of the war was that it drew people together. The situation inspired people to help one another in ways that are practically unheard of today. As Dave and Jean reflect on their memories of the war, they admit that while it was happening, they did not comprehend the magnitude of the situation. Jean states, "Being as young as we were, kids adjust. And that's just what you do. You know, this is life. It just doesn't stir you like the older people, except, as we grew older, it became more real to us—as we grew older, more serious."

# BIBLIOGRAPHY

Anderson, Jean "DeDe" Barnard. Interview by Danae Brentzel, July 3, 2003, Pittsburgh, PA.

Antanovich, Alex, Jr. Interview by David Scott Breveridge, June 26, 2005, Pittsburgh, PA.

Bates, Charles. Interview by Stephanie J. Fetsko, June 5, 2007, Pittsburgh, PA.

Bernstein, Sidney. Interview by Rocco Ross, June 30, 2007, Pittsburgh, PA.

Book, Raymond T. Interview by Stephanie J. Fetsko, June 6, 2007, Pittsburgh, PA.

Campbell, Edward and Rose. Interviewed by Justin Hoffman, July 14, 2005, Pittsburgh, PA.

Gruber, Bill. Interviewed by Sandy Doyle, June 5, 2007, Pittsburgh, PA.

Haberman, John and Sally. Interview by Heather Newell, May 24, 2003, Pittsburgh, PA.

Krebs, Helen McGrogan. Interviewed by Helen Krebs, June 12, 2002, Pittsburgh, PA.

Martin, Richard Charles. Interview by Jo Ellen Aleshire, June 1, 2007, Pittsburgh, PA.

Mulholland, Nora. Interview by Marian Mulholland, June 10, 2007, Pittsburgh, PA.

Price, David and Jean. Interview by Jennifer Welsh, June 27, 2008, Pittsburgh, PA.

Seifert, Frederick T. Interview by Karan Kranz, June 6, 2003, Pittsburgh, PA.

# INDEX

## T

trains  24, 25, 26, 34, 70, 83, 84, 85,
    90, 107, 137, 140
Truman, Harry S  29, 39, 73, 126

## U

U-boats  84
Uptown  69
USS *Franklin*  147, 148
USS *Franklin D. Roosevelt*  84, 86, 87
USS *Haan*  63
USS *Missouri*  15
USS *Phelps*  84
U.S. Steel  30

## V

V-E Day  38
victory garden  23, 49, 135, 149
V-J Day  39

## W

war bonds  14, 22, 34, 121, 129,
    140, 145, 151
war production  10, 24, 34, 36, 123
War Revenue Act of 1942  14
Westinghouse  14, 22, 23, 24, 27
West Newton  106

## Y

Youghiogheny River  131

# ABOUT THE EDITOR

A native of Pittsburgh's Shadyside neighborhood, Joseph F. Rishel is a descendant of Pennsylvania Dutch pioneers who came to America in 1738 and settled in western Pennsylvania after the War of 1812. He earned his PhD in history from the University of Pittsburgh. Dr. Rishel is a professor of history at Duquesne University, where he has taught for twenty-six years. He has written *Founding Families of Pittsburgh: The Evolution of a Regional Elite, 1760–1910* and *"The Spirit That Gives Life": A History of Duquesne University, 1878–1996* and has edited *American Cities and Towns: Historical Perspectives.* He now lives in Whitehall Borough in the South Hills of Pittsburgh with his wife, Helen. They are the parents of Jonathan, Emily, Marjorie and Elizabeth Rishel.

Visit us at
www.historypress.net